WAYS OF ESCAPE

An Outsider in Spain

NIGEL HAMSON

Text copyright ©2017 Nigel Hamson

The author has asserted his moral right under the Copyright, Designs and Patents Act, 1988, to be identified as the author of this work.

All rights reserved. No part of this publication may be reproduced, stored in a retrieval system, or transmitted, in any form or by any means, without the prior permission in writing of the publisher.

1

Even after a week in the village no-one knew exactly where he came from or what he was doing there. Those who were interested, most people between the ages of nine and ninety-eight (the oldest resident), knew that he was British, and a few knew that his name was Nigel Hamson, but only because of the passport which he had reluctantly relinquished to the owner of the small hotel, who had made a photocopy and returned it to his outstretched hand.

"You stay long... Neegel?" the owner had asked him in his broken English, his pronunciation of the G suggesting that he was preparing to spit.

"I don't know. I think so. Extremadura is very big," he had replied in carefully enunciated Spanish, before smiling and raising his hands wide to indicate great expanses of land. "Neegel," he said, as if to himself.

"It your name, yes? Neegel?"

"Sí, eso es. You pronounce it perfectly."

The hotel in the large village quite near to the historic town of Plasencia was empty apart from Nigel, whose plain first-floor room overlooked the pretty square. Despite the warm spring weather he spent an astonishing amount of time in that room over the following week, only leaving it to take a short walk around the village every day. He nodded solemnly to everyone he saw, before visiting a grocer's shop where he filled a small rucksack with bread, cheese and cold meats – the shop assistant said – which he consumed in his room, never leaving so much as a crumb or a scrap of paper, the hotel chambermaid asserted.

"He must only drink water from the tap," the shop assistant told the chambermaid, for they were cousins and also friends.

"He ought to eat more fruit and vegetables," said the chambermaid, whose name was Ana.

"Yes, he looks a little pale," said María, the shop assistant. "He isn't tall for a foreigner."

"No, but strong, and quite handsome with those blue eyes. How old do you think he is?"

"He is thirty-one. Eusebio told me," she said, referring to the owner of the hotel where her friend worked.

"He looks a little younger."

"Yes, he appears to have no worries. His expression is always calm. I wonder why he's here."

"I expect he will leave soon and we'll never know," said Ana. "He always smiles pleasantly when he leaves his room so that I can clean it, but he never speaks, or only to say hola."

"I think that is when he comes to the shop."

"Yes, that would make sense."

"At around eleven?" María asked.

"That's right. He always takes his little blue bag, so I expect he takes his rubbish and puts it in a bin. I never find any in the room, not even the little sachets of shampoo and gel, though I know that he showers daily."

After concluding that he must deposit his rubbish in the bin to the left of the church doors, María suggested that Ana check it on her way back to the hotel from her home.

"But why?" said Ana with a laugh, before collecting her long dark hair in her fist and slowly releasing it.

"I'm joking. There is no doubt that he uses that bin."

Almost exactly one week after Nigel's arrival a letter arrived for him. Ana took the thick envelope to his room when she called at the by now prearranged time of eleven o'clock. After the third day Nigel had always been ready to leave at this time, and he thanked her for the letter as they passed in the doorway.

"I hope it is good news," Ana said in Spanish.

"Yes, I think it is."

While Ana made the bed and tidied the spotless room she thought about Nigel, or Neegel, as he was yet to pronounce his name to anyone in the village, either correctly or incorrectly. Ana was twenty-eight and had never had a proper boyfriend. She had always avoided sleeping with any of the local boys, partly because her own birth had followed a shotgun wedding when her mother was seventeen, though her parents had got along fine since then. Having preserved her chastity in order to save herself for a nice young man, despite the teasing of her friends, she was now beginning to feel like an old maid.

Most of her friends had married the eligible men who had passed her by and she felt that her life was in something of a rut. She was still pretty and the fullness of her figure was an asset rather than otherwise, so she hoped to meet a man from out of town one day in the not too distant future. For this reason she was even more interested in Nigel than the other villagers, though as his days of solitude mounted up she began to think him a little strange. Still, she lingered in the room, patting the pillows and adjusting the curtains, as she intended to leave as soon as she heard him climbing the stairs.

That day, however, Nigel didn't return to his room until eleven o'clock in the evening. He was spotted on the bus to Plasencia at midday and it was assumed that he had returned the same way, though that left two hours unaccounted for, so he might have returned by taxi. Although Nigel had a key, Eusebio had waited for him behind his reception desk, where he had a small television and other comforts.

"Hola, Neegel. Has estado en Plasencia?" Eusebio asked, having realised by this time that he might not like being addressed in English, as the few foreign tourists who came in summer enjoyed practising their Spanish.

"Sí. Buenas noches."

Had Eusebio not been sipping brandy for the last hour, he would have detected a slight smell of alcohol on Nigel's breath, but as his nostrils were impervious to it, he put the young man's rosy cheeks down to the fresh air that he had shunned for so long until today.

"Will you be staying for much longer?" he asked the receding figure.

"Yes, I think so. Hasta mañana," he said, turning briefly and waving his hand.

As Nigel had paid for the week on the third day of his stay, Eusebio, an unusually thin man in his sixties, resolved not to mention further payment until his guest did. Normally tourists bored him and he preferred chatting to the travelling salesmen and businessmen who came regularly, but this one was beginning to intrigue him. He suspected that the fat letter which he had pawed that morning had contained money, or maybe a letter and a cheque, which would explain the trip to Plasencia, so he looked forward to seeing a change in his guest's hermit-like behaviour over the coming days.

The following day Nigel boarded the early morning bus along with several villagers who worked in Plasencia. He returned on the midday bus and walked to the hotel carrying a black travel bag which seemed quite heavy, as two men in the bar near the church saw him passing it from hand to hand.

"He is staying," said Bernardo, a retired farm worker.

"It appears so," said Esteban, a heavyset man of fifty. He had taken over the bar from his father, who now sat at a corner table playing dominos with another old-timer.

"The foreigner?" he asked his son.

"Sí, Papá. He has a new bag."

"May it make him happy," the old man said in a hoarse voice. "Why do these tourists come here?"

"They like the old towns and the wide spaces," said Esteban from the bar. "From here some of them also go up to the Sierra de Gredos, or so Eusebio tells me."

"When I was young there was nothing but suffering in these damn wide spaces."

"I know, Papá, but the tourists like to see the churches and palaces that the conquistadors built for us," he said, smiling at his friend Bernardo.

"Ha! Fat lot of good they did us." His father's sharp eyes scanned the area beside his table. "I would spit on the floor if it weren't so damn clean."

"I wonder what he has in the bag," said Bernardo after sipping his wine. "It is unusual for a tourist to buy more luggage once he is here."

"Maybe he isn't a tourist. Not all foreigners are tourists. Perhaps he has some purpose in mind," said Esteban.

"He will be selling something, you'll see," said the old man who sat opposite Esteban's father. He too had worked on the land, as had his companion until he had opened the bar in the 1970s. They were both over eighty and had been small children during the Civil War, though nothing awful had happened in the village. They had grown up during the years of scarcity and were still obsessed by money, while their wives were obsessed by food and still made their families and guests eat more than they wanted to.

"I hope he comes in here sometime," said Esteban as he wiped a glass with a white towel.

"If he goes anywhere, he will go to Fernando's," said Bernardo, referring to the only real restaurant in the village. "The tourists always do."

"I don't think he's a tourist," said Esteban. "Papá, go home to your lunch."

"One more game," he said, swirling the dominos around on the table.

Nigel didn't go out again that day, despite the warm sunshine which many of the villagers were enjoying after the especially long, cold winter. Both Eusebio and Ana walked past his room several times and sometimes heard shuffling sounds, as if he were unpacking or arranging things. Ana returned after lunch at home, just to see if any more guests were due to arrive.

"Yes, thank God. Federico, the salesman from Seville, will be staying for two nights. I think we'll put him in the room next to the Englishman's."

"But there's no need. There are eleven empty rooms."

"I am aware of that, Ana, but he might hear something interesting. Also, as you know, Federico is very talkative. He may be able to draw out our mysterious stranger, if he sees him."

"Very well. I'll prepare number three."

"But Neegel's bathroom is between the two. Please prepare number one."

"OK. Ha, you use his name as if you were friends!"

"Neegel isn't an ordinary guest," he said, scratching his scrawny neck and shrugging.

The following morning at eleven o'clock Nigel said more than two or three words to Ana for the first time. He was dressed in a beige-coloured suit that was so light as to be almost white, a light-blue shirt, a pink tie, and very shiny brown shoes. Such was Ana's surprise that she had to ask him to repeat what he had said.

"I would like to move to another room, if possible," he said.

"Oh, did the other guest disturb you?"

"Not at all, but I have been in this room for nine days now and I would like to move to the second floor," he said slowly, pronouncing each word deliberately and well.

"Well, there are three rooms up there with views of the square, but they are larger rooms, one with a double bed, and two with two single beds," she said, unable to take her eyes off his elegant clothes.

"May I have the room with the double bed?"

"Yes, unless it's booked for the weekend, which I doubt. It's more expensive though."

"That isn't a problem. I am ready to move," he said, pointing to his two packed travel bags and his little blue rucksack. "The smaller black bag contains dirty clothes. Does the hotel have a laundry?"

"A lady in the village washes and irons the clothes of our guests. If you like I can take the bag and return it with clean clothes tomorrow."

"Thank you."

"Are you sure the other guest didn't disturb you?" she asked, smiling for the first time and keen to continue the conversation.

"Not at all. It is true that I prefer to be… isolated, but I know that as the weather improves more guests will arrive."

"So are you planning to stay for a long time?"

"I think so. I like the village."

"But you never go out, except to the shop and to Plasencia! I expect you are going there now, as you are dressed so smartly."

"Oh no, I have concluded my business there. Now I will stay in the village."

"In your room?"

"No. So, may I move, Ana?"

His use of her name made her blush, as they had never introduced themselves. "I'll just go and ask Eusebio, the owner."

"Yes, it is free. Did he talk to you?" asked Eusebio, who had been standing outside in the sun, quite close to Nigel's window.

"A little. I will get the key."

"Try to find out more about him."

"Shall I ask him to pay? He owes two nights already."

Eusebio smoothed back his thinning hair. "No, say nothing about that for now."

When Ana returned to the first floor he was nowhere to be seen. She checked that his room was empty and walked up the stairs, where he was waiting with his bags outside the double room.

"You guessed the room," she said.

"I sensed it was the correct one."

She opened the door and led the way inside. "It's the best room in the hotel, but I should have prepared it first. I wasn't thinking." She opened the curtains, pulled up the blind, and opened the windows. "Ah, that's nice. You ought to go outside more," she said as she turned to face him.

"Why is it that you aren't married, Ana?"

This time her blush was tremendous and she was lost for words.

"I'm sorry, I shouldn't have asked, but I noticed you weren't wearing a ring. Also you aren't so old. I'm sure you have a boyfriend." He said this with a benign expression on his pale, untroubled face. Ana noticed that his light brown hair almost touched his clear blue eyes and also curled up under his ears.

"No I don't have a boyfriend at the moment," she said with a nervous smile.

"Yes, you are right, I need a haircut. Could you tell me where there is a barber's?"

"Yes." As she gave him directions she became calmer and thought that his reference to her ringless finger wasn't so unusual. Some of the regular guests liked to banter with her, so why shouldn't he? He hadn't asked the question in a joking way like them, however, and she noticed that he wore no rings at all.

"Thank you, Ana. I will look smarter when I have had a haircut."

"You look very smart already in those clothes. That's why I thought you were going to Plasencia."

"No. Hasta luego, Ana."

"Adiós… Neegel. Oh, I will take the bag with your clothes."

"Gracias, Ana."

"Did you see that suit?" Eusebio asked her when she went downstairs half an hour later.

"How could I miss it? He's gone to have a haircut."

"Did he say anything to you?"

"No, nothing interesting. Oh, he says he won't be returning to Plasencia, and that he plans to stay for some time. He says he likes the village."

"What? The hotel and the shop?"

"And now Roberto's."

"Ha, Roberto will extract some information, I'm sure. He is gifted in that way."

"Yes, he's the biggest gossip in the village," Ana said, glancing down at her fingers.

Roberto the barber extracted no information whatsoever from Nigel, who after asking him to cut his hair very short replied to each of his prying questions briefly, before asking a question of his own. Roberto and Esteban had been to school together and the barber told the bar owner that the forastero, or stranger, had asked him about all four eateries in the village, and seemed especially interested in Fernando's restaurant.

"Damn it, I knew he would end up going there. They all do. What kind of questions did he ask?"

Roberto, a short man, drank from his small bottle of beer and tipped his bald head from side to side. Some hair still grew around his head, but due to the nature of his trade he preferred to shave it twice a week. "He asked about the food on offer and about the type of clientele that frequents each one."

"What did you tell him about this place?"

"That it was similar to the other two bars, but that you had the best tapas and bocadillos."

"Thank you."

"One must always lie for one's friends. I also told him that Fernando's restaurant has a more varied clientele and that the tourists who visit here usually go there."

"Oh, then—"

Roberto lifted a chubby index finger. "This had the desired effect. I had guessed that the man was one of those tourists who thinks he isn't a tourist. You know, the ones who try to speak Spanish and pick up the newspaper and pretend to read it."

"But this one speaks Spanish, doesn't he?"

"Yes, this one does, slowly but correctly, as if he had learnt it at school. Anyway, as I told him about the delights of Fernando's cuisine and his multinational patrons, I saw a disdainful look in his eyes, or at least I think I did."

"He will go there. What else did he ask you?"

"Oh, about the shops, the church, the library, the school."

"The school? Why the school?"

"I don't know. He asked at what age the children started there and if it was a good school. I told him it was just fine for us and then asked him if he had any young children. Do you know what he replied?"

"What?"

"Maybe. He said maybe, before asking me if it were possible to hire a car in the village. I told him about Juan's garage."

"Juan's clandestine garage, yes, but what a strange answer to your question about children."

"Yes, but there was no way to clarify that without being rude, and it's possible that 'maybe' wasn't the word he intended to say. Besides, by that time I had cut off most of his hair and he was about to leave. He looks like a soldier now," he laughed, before shaking his head. "I got most of the hairs off his suit."

"A suit?"

Roberto told him about Nigel's clothing, so they talked about that until he finished his beer and went home for lunch.

Meanwhile, Nigel was eating at a small table in Fernando's restaurant. Despite thirteen of the sixteen tables being free, he had chosen one in a corner far from the bar, much to the annoyance of Eduardo, the young but ponderous waiter. Eduardo liked walking even less than he liked working in the restaurant, a job that he had drifted into after school but which had kept him in work through the economic slump, making him the envy of his more ambitious peers. Eduardo didn't show the slightest interest in Nigel, simply taking his order for the set lunch menu, before fetching each item as coolly as a Parisian waiter whose instinct tells him his tip will be negligible. It was, therefore, curious that Nigel ended up telling this dull-eyed young man much more about himself than anyone else he had spoken to in the village.

Up until coffee time Nigel had merely thanked him for each indolent delivery, but on receiving his café solo he asked Eduardo to sit down for a moment. This was rather irregular, but what could the young sluggard do but obey his customer? He was glad of the chance to rest his corpulent body and there would be time enough to explain matters to Fernando, whose hawkish eyes he felt boring into his back.

"I am Neegel. Pleased to meet you," he said with a winning smile, before thrusting out his hand.

"Likewise," said the waiter, allowing his hand to be shaken.

"I will be staying at the hotel for some time."

"Oh," he said, being one of the few people who had known nothing of Nigel's existence.

"I think this village is rather special, don't you?"

"It's all right."

"I have great plans, so many plans that I hardly know where to begin." He smiled brightly, his suit and new haircut making him look like an especially zealous Mormon missionary, despite the pink tie. "Do you think, for instance, that a really excellent restaurant would work here?"

"Er, well, my uncle thinks this one is excellent," he said, nodding towards Fernando, who often rued his familial connections, especially the one he had reluctantly agreed to employ almost a decade earlier. Nine times out of ten he would have barked out an order at this point, but this foreigner was a special case, so he withdrew to the kitchen in order not to cramp his nephew's style, such as it was.

"Yes, yes, it's fine, but I mean a really good one. You know, one that might get a Michelin star." His blue eyes bored into the hapless lad's rather bovine brown ones. "One that people would come to from Madrid, Barcelona and even Paris."

"I don't know."

"Or what about a luxury hotel? Do you think that would be successful? Do many tourists come here?"

"Some, in summer, especially in August," he said, feeling slightly more relaxed on seeing that his employer and uncle – in that order – was no longer eyeballing him. His slow mind had also realised that after this little interview he might have something to say for himself for once in his life, as he recalled that his fiancée María, Ana's cousin, had mentioned something about a new face in town, though he had been watching the football at the time.

"Hmm, I'll have to think some more about it. I have money to invest, you see, and I'm enchanted by this place. Ha, I suppose if you are from here, you see it as quite an ordinary village."

"Yes."

"But I think it's perfect. I think that now that the worst of the economic slump is over, Extremadura is really going to take off as a tourist destination. Don't you agree?"

"I don't know." The impending tip that this smart stranger might give him had just crossed his mind and he dug deep into his mostly fallow brain for something interesting to say. "It's very quiet here and there is a lot of countryside. Some tourists like that."

"Exactly!" Nigel slapped the table. "It's good to talk to someone who really knows the place. What's your name again?"

"Eduardo."

"Eduardo, but please don't mention our conversation to anyone just yet. I'll be coming here quite often from now on and…" He tapped his nose. "Maybe a young chap like you will form part of my plans. I mean, it must be a bit boring just working here."

"A bit, sometimes," he said. The set menu cost ten euros with coffee, so he thought that this weird guy ought to be good for five more.

"You've got potential, I can see that, but not a word to anyone just yet," he said. Throughout the conversation he had been speaking increasingly quickly, until he sounded almost fluent, but the reappearance of the owner made him revert to his more pedestrian speech. "It has been nice speaking to you, Eduardo. Could I have my bill, please?"

Eduardo nodded and pushed himself up from his chair with remarkable celerity, before marching to the bar for no reason at all as he knew that the bill was ten euros. As he approached his uncle he pursed his lips in a thoughtful way and saw from the older man's bulging eyes that the stranger's secrets would be safe for no more than two minutes once he had left the restaurant.

"Eduardo told me that he said he was going to set up a luxury hotel or restaurant in the village," María told Ana the next afternoon as they drank coffee in Esteban's bar, out of earshot in the corner.

"Really?"

"Yes, and he gave him a ten euro tip," she said, her brown eyes flashing; eyes that were far less dull than her boyfriend's and reflected the livelier portion of grey matter which she had been allotted, but she was a homely girl and hadn't wanted to end up on the shelf like her older cousin. "It sounds like he's got a lot of money."

"Yes," Ana said, before lowering her eyes and stroking her smooth cheeks with her middle finger and thumb.

"What?"

"Oh, this morning I went to his room at eleven and he was just about to leave, as usual. When I told him that his laundry would be back this afternoon he thanked me and left," she said with a frown.

"And?"

"Yesterday he spoke to me for longer and... well, we chatted," she said, deciding not to mention his comments regarding her marital status. There was enough gossip in the village already and she didn't wish to form part of it, though María was usually discreet. "Anyway, while I was cleaning his room I spotted a cheque on his bedside table and I couldn't help looking at it."

"Naughty girl."

"I know, but it was just there. It was for €40,000, payable to him."

"Really? Who was it from?"

"I didn't look. I know it was from a foreign bank, but I turned it over."

"I bet he left it there on purpose."

"Possibly. It's a lot of money."

"I could write you a cheque for a million euros, Ana. Anyone can write a cheque."

"I suppose so, but it fits in with what he told your Edu. I wonder why he decided to talk to him."

"Maybe he spotted his brilliance when he walked through the door," said María with a giggle. "Poor Edu, he didn't know what to make of the man, and then his uncle interrogated him for the next half hour."

"Has he eaten there again today?"

"I don't think so. I told Edu to send me a text if he did."

As the young women chatted, Nigel was drinking coffee in the bar on the main road, after eating from the cheap, cheerful and mostly tasteless daily menu. The owner, a buxom lady in her forties called Sara, had served him and at first assumed he was passing through, as his smart appearance didn't fit the description she had of the mysterious foreigner. The village grapevine was thorough, but updates sometimes took as long as forty-eight hours to take effect.

"This is a pretty village," Nigel said to her between the passable stew and the insipid chicken and chips.

"Yes, where are you heading?"

"Nowhere. I'm staying at the hotel here," he said in his speedy Spanish. The only other diners were six workmen in matching overalls who he guessed were from elsewhere.

"Ah." She nodded. "Are you comfortable there?"

"Perfectly. Eusebio is a pleasant man and Ana, the chambermaid, is a charming young lady," he said with slightly dreamy eyes.

"Yes, she is a good girl, but…"

"What?"

"Well, she could do better than work there. Her hours are few, apart from in summer, and… oh, I must attend to the other table. Excuse me."

Now as he stirred his coffee in the empty restaurant, his periodic glances at Sara made it clear that he wished to continue their conversation. After clearing the workmen's table she asked him if he wanted anything else.

"Just a moment of you time, if I may," he said, before sliding out the chair beside him. This was almost as irregular as his invitation to Eduardo the previous day, but she was the owner – her husband was a lorry driver – and it would give her and Elena, her cook and niece, something to talk about later. She sat down and smoothed down her apron. Nigel just smiled and looked at her benevolently.

"So... are you staying in the village for long?" she asked when it became clear that he wasn't going to speak.

"Yes, that is my plan. I am Neegel." He extended his hand and squeezed her chubby fingers gently and briefly.

"I'm Sara." She felt her face reddening. "This is my bar."

"I know. Eusebio told me about it."

"Did he?" she asked with surprise.

"Yes, we were discussing rural tourism, you see, and this place cropped up."

"Oh. Why?"

"Well, I'm thinking about buying property in the country in order to build rural accommodation for tourists. Small chalets, perhaps, or maybe I will buy a farmhouse and divide it up."

"I'm not sure any are for sale."

"Everybody has their price," he said flatly, though his eyes were smiling.

"And where does my bar come into it?"

"Oh, perhaps as a point of contact when I meet the investors."

"Investors?"

"Yes, it will be a very expensive undertaking. I cannot do it alone. Tell me, do you know the politicians in the village?"

"Yes, there's Enrique, the mayor, and I know the other councillors, but they normally leave everything to him."

"Why's that?"

"Well, he's been mayor for a long time and people trust him. It's a quiet village, you see, and nothing much happens. When Enrique got funding for the new sports centre and swimming pool everybody was very happy, so... well, they let him get on with it."

"Is he a greedy man?" he murmured, though they were still alone.

"What?" Her eyes widened, then narrowed in thought, before returning to their normal aperture. Nigel's eyes continued to gaze at her. "No, I don't think he's greedy at all. Why do you ask?"

He shrugged his broad shoulders. "Oh, I don't know. I still don't know how things work here. Where could I meet him?"

"He's at the Casa Consistorial some evenings, though he works as a digger driver."

"A digger driver? What a strange job for a mayor!"

"He refuses payment for his village duties."

"So he isn't at all corrupt?"

"No, not at all," she said, sounding annoyed. She began to rise, but he raised his right hand a few inches from the table, so she stayed put, her hands still gripping the seat of her chair.

"I'm sorry if I offended you by asking such questions about the mayor, but I had to be sure."

"About what?"

"That he is an honest man. I know there is a lot of corruption in Spain and that some businessmen like it, as it enables them to get what they want more easily, but me and the other investors only work with reputable councils. My colleagues are Dutch, Swedish and Danish, you see, and they are all very strict men." He sipped his tepid coffee and smiled.

"And where are you from, Neegel?"

"I am British, though my mother is Swedish and my father was German."

"How interesting? How did you all end up in Britain?"

"Oh, circumstances. I have lived in many different places, but now I wish to settle down."

"The village is a very dull place."

"Oh, I prefer quiet places. I am the type of person who makes his own entertainment. Could I have the bill, please, Sara?"

Sara brought him his bill for ten euros on a little plate. He thanked her and sipped his coffee, seeming lost in thought. When she stepped into the kitchen he placed a ten euro note on the plate and silently left the bar, even making sure that the door didn't bang shut.

That evening, dressed only in a scruffy polo shirt, old jeans and worn leather sandals, he slipped out of the hotel without seeing Eusebio and made his way to a small bar on a narrow street owned by a slovenly man called Victor. The more down-to-earth and sometimes boisterous men of the village gathered there most evenings to watch football on a huge TV screen, the only new thing in the much neglected bar. It was by far the worst place he could have chosen for a bite to eat.

Despite the warm spring days, the evenings were still cool up on the Extremaduran plain and his pale, bare arms caused most of the dozen or so men to turn from the screen to look at him. Eyes down, he found a stool right at the end of the bar and asked Victor, a red-faced, unhealthy-looking man with a large potbelly, for a coke and a ration of the revolting squid rings which he pointed to in the musty glass cabinet on the bar. The Spanish words left his mouth with great difficulty and he didn't seem to know the word for squid.

"Gracias," he said in a strong foreign accent, before tucking into the squid with apparent relish.

The men were watching an important European match with rapt attention. Nigel hadn't the slightest interest in football or any other sport, so he ate his squid with bread and sipped his coke. At half-time the other men ordered more beer or wine and chatted to each other in their mostly hoarse or gravelly voices, occasionally glancing at the quiet foreigner who seemed to be absorbed in an old calendar behind the bar. A small, oldish man who appeared a little the worse for drink approached Nigel and greeted him.

"Hola," he replied, glancing briefly at the man.

"You are staying at the hotel, I believe," he croaked, his artless face tanned and lined by the sun.

"Yes, I stay one night," he said slowly.

"Only tonight? I thought you had been there for a while."

"No, only tonight. With brother. He stay long time."

"But I'm sure I saw you yesterday, dressed in a nice suit."

"My brother. My brother and me, we…" He pointed to his face, opened his mouth, and shrugged.

"You are twins?"

"Yes, twins." Nigel smiled and nodded. "I buy drink. You want?"

"Let me buy you one. What would you like?"

"Small brandy, please."

"Right. Victor! Two cognacs here!"

Victor ambled over and poured two large brandies that certainly weren't French, but the man didn't seem to mind.

"Salud," he said, and took a sip.

"Salud," said Nigel, and drained his glass, before licking his lips in appreciation. "Victor, dos más, por favor."

Always happy to see his customers drinking freely, as he sold very little food apart from crisps, nuts and olives, Victor refilled his glass and held the bottle poised to refill the man's, which he was soon able to do.

"Salud," said Nigel, and downed his drink, before placing the glass on the bar and pointing to it. Victor refilled it with a shrug, but the man waved his finger, shook his head, and returned to his cronies, who had all been observing these wild west drinking antics with mute interest.

Nigel then drank his third brandy in two gulps, before requesting another, along with the bill, which he paid before nursing his full glass in silence for the entire second half. The Spanish team appeared to be winning and the men forgot about Nigel as they cheered, groaned or berated the referee. Nigel looked mostly at the calendar, but as the final whistle approached he slowly finished his drink and stood up.

"Yes!" he cried in English at the top of his voice when the match ended. "Yes, yes, yes!" he bellowed, completely beside himself with a kind of aggressive glee, punching the air with both fists as he spat out the words. He then rushed to the door without looking at anyone and ran down the street.

"He is a madman," said Victor to the astonished company.

"He is staying at the hotel," one man said. "Earlier he was wearing a suit."

"No, he isn't," said Nigel's erstwhile drinking companion. "He is his twin brother and is only staying for one night," he added, slurring his speech.

"The brother will be glad when he goes," said another man.

"Foreigners," said Victor, before switching off the television.

On turning the corner at the bottom of the street, Nigel came to a halt and looked up and down the slightly wider street which led to the church. As nobody was around he strolled back to the square and positioned himself behind an old stone pillar from where he could see part of Eusebio's recumbent figure. He apparently preferred his small TV in the reception to his larger one in his fine house on the edge of the village, where his wife awaited him. In August he sometimes stayed at the hotel until after eleven, but now there was no reason whatsoever to do so.

Nigel sat down on a bench in the shadows from where he could just see Eusebio's feet. He stayed there for about half an hour until they disappeared, whereupon he trotted over to the hotel and silently slipped through the door and up the stairs.

"Hello, brother," he said into the bathroom mirror, before cleaning his teeth, washing his face, undressing, and going to bed, where he read a short story by John Cheever before switching out the bedside light.

2

When Ana knocked on his door the next morning at exactly eleven o'clock, Nigel opened it and ushered her into the room, leaving the door open. He was wearing a grey fleece top, blue walking shorts, white socks, and new trainers.

"Buenos días, Ana. I am just going out," he said, observing her closely.

"To do some sport?"

"Not sport, but I will go for a walk in the country." He grabbed a red baseball cap from the bed.

"That's good. It's a lovely day and you ought to go out more."

"I know. I have been spending a lot of time in here because I had to finish some work," he said, pointing to a file and a large notebook that she hadn't seen before.

"Ah, about your business?" she asked, smiling.

"What business?" he asked sharply.

"Oh, I heard that you wanted to open a restaurant or something," she mumbled, feeling herself blush.

"Damn it, I only mentioned that to Eduardo at the restaurant. I told him not to tell anyone," he said, not sounding especially annoyed.

"Oh, Fernando, his uncle, will have made him tell. Edu isn't a very clever boy, you know."

"I know, that's why I told him that nonsense, just to see if anyone could keep a secret here."

"Oh."

"Ha, well, it's not exactly nonsense, as I have vague plans, but I haven't enough money to carry them out," he said, looking fixedly at the bedside table, empty now apart from a water glass.

"I see," Ana said, looking nervously out of the window.

"You saw that cheque, of course. I noticed you had turned it over."

She faced him and held his gaze. "I... I turned it over so as not to see it. You shouldn't have left it there."

"Oh, it doesn't matter." He smiled at her before stooping to adjust his laces.

"I don't need to clean your room every day, you know. There's a sign you can hang on the doorknob if you don't wish anyone to enter," she said as calmly as she could.

"Oh, I have no secrets, Ana, not from you anyway, though I would prefer you not to look in my folder and notebook."

"But why on earth would I look? I've cleaned all these rooms dozens of times and never looked at anyone's things," she said calmly, having decided that he was teasing her. He really was a preposterous man and in some ways she wished he would leave the village.

"But you will be curious," he said with a chuckle.

"Well, I will be now, of course, but I still won't look. You are very strange, Neegel."

"I like your voice, Ana, especially when you say my name. You have such a gentle voice, unlike most people here. Look." He took the notebook from the chair, opened it, and showed her two full pages.

"Your handwriting is very bad. It is English, no? Is it a story?"

"Well, it's more of a memoir. I have some free time now, so I decided to try writing something. I don't think it's much good." He closed the notebook and slipped it inside the folder. "Ana?"

"Yes."

"Oh, nothing. I'll go now and let you get on with your work. Thanks for the clean clothes by the way. When did you bring them?"

"I didn't. Eusebio brought them last night."

"Oh, do you know what time?"

"No, but Maribel, the woman who does the laundry, probably brought them round at about eight. She usually does. Is anything wrong?"

"What?" He turned his frown into a smile. "Oh, no, I was just thinking about my writing. If I don't see you before, I'll see you at eleven tomorrow. I may want to ask you something."

"What?"

"Hasta luego, Ana," he said, lifting his arm as if about to touch hers, before turning and striding out of the door.

About two and a half hours later Nigel entered Esteban's bar for the very first time, looking quite flushed after his long walk in the sun. He had headed north out of the village on a minor road, before taking a track through the pastureland dotted with holm-oak and cork-oak trees, though he didn't know their names. After walking towards the distant mountains for over an hour, he turned round and headed back the same way, taking his time and occasionally oinking at the fat black pigs he saw lumbering around beneath the trees. He also took a few photos on his phone, more or less at random.

Esteban didn't rub his hands together when Nigel walked in, but he looked as though he might. He knew that the foreigner had visited all the other bars, posing as his twin brother and behaving very oddly at Victor's last night. He had heard the twin story very early that morning, just after he had opened at six, in fact, but Eusebio had assured him later that he had seen Neegel leave the hotel in scruffy clothes and that his room had been empty when he had taken up the clean laundry some time later.

"Buenos días. What can I get you?"

"A large bottle of water and a glass, please. I am very thirsty," Nigel said, pitching his Spanish somewhere between his near fluency and the hesitant, heavily accented, rudimentary style that he sometimes chose to employ.

Esteban produced the water and the glass. "Are you enjoying your stay in our humble village?" he asked after checking that his father and his friend had stopped slapping down their dominoes and were paying attention. He expected his friend Bernardo to arrive any minute, so he resolved to utter commonplace things until then.

"Yes, I like it. This morning I walk in country. Nice trees. Nice pigs." He emptied his glass and refilled it.

"Those pigs eat only acorns, unless there are none. The best hams in Spain come from them." He looked through the door and saw Bernardo approaching, so he poured a glass of red wine in readiness.

"Yes, very fat pigs. Hola," Nigel said to the new arrival, who rubbed his hands together and hopped onto the stool beside him. "My name is Neegel," he said to Esteban, tendering his hand.

"Esteban, and this is Bernardo."

Hands were shaken and dominos were swirled over at the corner table, causing Esteban to look sharply at the old men, who were a little hard of hearing at the best of times.

"So, I believe you intend to promote rural tourism in this area," he said to Nigel.

"Me? Who says that?"

"Oh, it was mentioned. Also that you may set up a grand hotel or a luxury restaurant." His smiling brown eyes remained fixed on Nigel's as his head nodded almost imperceptibly.

"Ideas, just ideas," Nigel said with a tight-lipped smile, before drinking another glass of water.

"How is your brother?"

You could have heard a pin drop in the bar, which was most unusual, as the television was normally on all the time.

"My brother?"

"Yes, your twin brother who visited Victor's bar last night and enjoyed the football very much."

"I don't have brother. I have sister, but she lives in Quebec. She is a…" he searched for the word, "…midwife."

"Oh."

"Ha, I drink a lot last night. I remember I talk to one man, but my Spanish bad. He also very drunk."

Esteban had expected to have the foreigner squirming by this time, but in the event he was flummoxed and more inclined to squirm than Nigel, who had turned on his stool and was surveying the bar. Though he nodded at the old men, he seemed more interested in the fabric of the place than the people in it. He then walked to the door, opened it, and stepped outside, before walking slowly back to his stool, looking around him, but not at the four men.

"Can I have lunch here?" he asked Esteban when he had sat down again.

"Er, yes, we have some lamb stew and I can make you hake and chips," he said, as so few people ate there that his daily menu was almost non-existent.

"And salad?"

"Yes."

"May I sit over there?" He pointed to the table furthest away from the old men, although they were now preparing to leave.

"Yes."

"May I take the newspaper?"

"Yes," he said, handing over that day's Periódico de Extremadura. "To drink?"

"I will take my bottle of water."

Between two and three was almost always the quietest time of day for Esteban, as even Bernardo had to go home to eat with his wife. As the foreigner seemed disinclined to talk, he switched on the television, the eerie hush having unnerved him, and tried to stop looking over at his strange customer. He then busied himself in the kitchen and Nigel thanked him politely when each dish was brought, before returning his gaze to the provincial news pages. Bernardo returned at about a quarter past three, along with a couple of younger men in faded blue overalls, and Esteban greeted them exuberantly, before pushing, pulling and banging the coffee machine with great energy. He joked with one of the men about his noisy tractor, but when Nigel approached the bar their conversation died away.

He sat on the same stool, next to Bernardo, and handed the folded newspaper to Esteban. "Thank you. I will take coffee here. A cortado, please." He looked at Bernardo. "Do you also work in the country?"

"I used to. I'm retired now, but I still attend to my piece of land and a few chickens."

"I may buy a small house and a little land here sometime soon, and also have a few animals," he said, now in his fluent Spanish.

"Oh."

"But I will have to ask for a lot of advice, as I'm really a city person."

"Right," said Bernardo, sipping his coffee and looking at Esteban for help.

"Which cities have you lived in?" he duly asked.

"London, Quebec and Melbourne," he said, smiling at him and Bernardo. "Madrid too, but only for a short time."

"Whereabouts?" asked Esteban.

"Near the Castellana, at a small hotel. I met some interesting people in the city. They are filmmakers from Germany and wish to make a film about rural life in Spain. I came here more or less at random, but I promised to tell them if I ended up in a place that might be suitable for their film."

"And have you?" asked Bernardo.

"I think so. They want to make a documentary about village and country life. I think this would be the best bar in which to film some of the conversational scenes, or maybe Fernando's restaurant."

"Not Victor's bar, or Sara's?" asked Esteban with a cynical smile.

"Ha, not Victor's! I made a fool of myself there last night and am ashamed to go back. I'm not used to drinking, you see, and I lost my head."

"Sara's is a nice village bar," Esteban said.

"It is, and I enjoyed my lunch there, though the food wasn't as good as yours, but for the film I envision a man behind the bar, rather than a woman. I think it's what the viewers would expect. Of course, if you would rather they didn't film here…"

"Oh, I don't mind. Papá," he called to his father, who had just entered and was approaching his domino table. "I may be on television. Do you think I'd look good on television?"

"You would break the camera. Are you making a film, young man?"

"Some friends of mine."

Bernardo then filled in the old man about the nature of the film, without a trace of irony in his voice.

"Ha, then they must interview me and old Jose Ramón. We know more about the country than anyone here."

"Yes, I'm sure they would wish to do that."

"Then tell them to hurry. I might be dead soon," he said, still standing in the middle of the bar, much wrinkled by the sun but lean and upright.

"Oh, don't say that, señor. I'm sure you have many more years left to live."

"Neegel, will you permit me to make an observation?" asked Esteban, seeming to hold in his ample stomach as he polished a glass.

"Go ahead, Esteban."

"When you arrived today your Spanish wasn't very good, but now you speak very well. Why is that, if you don't mind me asking?"

"Oh, timidity. I have only learnt Spanish during the last few months, and when I feel nervous, like when I meet new people, I can't seem to get the words out."

"Very curious."

"I also find that I speak better on a full stomach, though I don't know why."

"Right," said Esteban, nonplussed, but not for long. "Tell me, do you also speak French, having lived in Quebec?" he asked, now permitting himself a guileful glance at Bernardo and the other two men at the bar.

"Je le parle, mais pas très bien. J'ai vécu avec ma sœur pendant environ un an quand j'étais adolescent," he said quickly. "But I am losing it now, little by little," he added in Spanish. "Now I must go. Combien je te dois, Esteban?"

"Qué?"

"Sorry, I thought you spoke French, as you asked me if I did. How much do I owe you?"

"Just ten."

"Here, thank you. Oh, that reminds me, I must pay my hotel bill. Your friend Eusebio will think me very rude. We will meet again soon. Adiós, adiós," he said to the company, before strolling happily through the door.

As may be imagined, Nigel was discussed thoroughly that afternoon. Esteban's father thought him charming and a breath of fresh air in a village that was even duller than when he was a boy. Bernardo had been so impressed by his French, and especially by the way he had caught Esteban out, that any inconsistencies paled into insignificance. Esteban thought there was something very fishy about him, very fishy indeed, but he was intrigued by his news about the German film crew and rather hoped they would come.

"A German film crew?" Eusebio asked at about six o'clock, after receiving a full news bulletin.

"That's what he said," said Esteban, scratching his heavy, stubbly jaw. "Though I'm not sure if I believe anything he says. Did he pay his hotel bill earlier?"

"No, he hasn't been back to the hotel."

"You see? He said he was going to. If I were you I'd ask him for payment soon. That type of person could just up and disappear."

"Hmm, yes, I'll mention it to him later," said Eusebio, whose wife was pleased to have seen so little of him over the last few days. It was almost like summer, when she could watch whatever she chose on television.

Nigel hadn't gone back to the hotel because he had changed his mind. Instead he visited the other three bars, spending about an hour in each. His Spanish was middling to good, but he spoke very little as he sipped his water, making no reference to his twin brother in Victor's bar, or to his hotel and restaurant ambitions at Fernando's, or to his rural tourism project at Sara's. The only thing he told the three owners, in fact, was that a German film crew would be coming soon to make a documentary and that they might wish to film some conversations in their bar. All three acquiesced, of course, and Victor said that he'd been thinking of giving his place a lick of paint for some time.

Nigel strolled back to the hotel at about half past nine and told Eusebio that he wished to pay what he owed and for another two weeks.

"That way I won't forget to pay," he said with a chuckle.

"As you wish," said Eusebio, before prodding an old white calculator for some time.

On hearing the rather large amount, Nigel took out his wallet and extracted two €200 and a few €100 notes, before handing them to Eusebio.

"I will write you a receipt."

"It isn't necessary. Buenas noches, Eusebio."

"Buenas noches, y gracias," he replied. He examined the notes carefully when Nigel had climbed the stairs. They looked fine, but he would take them to the bank first thing tomorrow. He too hoped that the German filmmakers would come, as his was the only hotel in the village. A man of wealth, he reflected, could be permitted a little eccentricity, and he was glad that Neegel was staying on. If nothing else, it made him a more important figure in the village and people no longer looked so bored when he entered a bar or other establishment. People even called in to see him in reception occasionally, something they had rarely done before.

After writing in his notebook for a while, Nigel lay back on his bed with his hands under his head. On the whole he was pleased with his progress, though it was a shame that the twin brother business hadn't come off. There was still something missing though, something he doubted he would find by trailing round the bars. There must be about two thousand people in the village and he guessed that only a couple of hundred of them visited the bars with much regularity. He sat up and opened his notebook again.

"So far I have only seen the tip of the iceberg and tomorrow I must spread my net wider," he wrote, before crossing out the ridiculous imagery and trying again.

3

The next morning Ana was surprised to see the *Por Favor, No Molestar* sign hanging from Neegel's doorknob. Eusebio had said nothing about him having left the hotel and she lingered for a minute, hoping to hear signs of life. He had been going to ask her something too, and she was intrigued about that, but she couldn't knock on the door, so she took her cleaning things down to the first floor where two rooms were now occupied.

Nigel had in fact left the hotel at seven o'clock and gone for another walk. He headed roughly south this time and enjoyed the vast views, and although he saw some cattle and a few goats he was disappointed not to see any more pigs. Pigs were funny, inquisitive animals, rather like humans in many ways, and he thought he would rather like to own some one day. He took photos of two farmhouses that he passed and returned to the village at nine. After a light breakfast at Sara's, chosen because she was the least inquisitive of the bar owners, he visited a nearby bakery and bought a baguette. He exchanged a few pleasantries with the middle-aged lady there in the almost fluent Spanish that he had decided to use from now on. This was all new to him, after all, and he was happy to jettison strategies that promised to be fruitless, though strategy might be too precise a word for so open-ended an undertaking as Nigel's.

He then visited a small supermarket that he had previously eschewed in favour of the grocer's shop where Ana's cousin María worked. He popped some shoe polish, toothpaste and a box of energy bars into his basket, before approaching the checkout. There were two women working, one in her fifties and the other of about twenty, so he chose the older woman and remarked that he hadn't needed a basket after all.

"Ha, no, you have few things," she said pleasantly.

"That noticeboard over there beside the door. May I put a little message on it?"

"Of course. That's what it is for."

"I'm looking for a house in the village, you see, and I thought I might announce that… well, ask if anyone is selling one. I'm staying at the hotel at the moment."

"Ah," she said. This lady wasn't particularly fond of gossip, but she had heard about the strange foreigner. Generally speaking, the twin episode was of little interest, as people took anything reported by the patrons of Victor's bar with a pinch of salt, but his entrepreneurial schemes were much discussed and the German film crew story was also beginning to do the rounds. "Do you wish to buy a house, or just rent one?"

"Oh, I hadn't thought of renting one," he said, looking momentarily gormless, something his red baseball cap made easier. "I suppose that might be the best idea."

"Yes, it's better at first, I think. This is a dull village."

"That's why I like it. I want a quiet life. Thank you for your help."

"De nada," she said with a smile, having taken a liking to the modest, rather awkward young man. People really did jump to the most unfair conclusions, she thought as she watched him open the door for an elderly lady.

On a quiet street Nigel scrunched up the baguette and dropped it into a bin, before entering another bakery and buying some croissants. From there he proceeded to the library and made a mental note of the two mornings and evenings when it was open, before spotting a tiny shop along the street that turned out to be a haberdashery. On opening the creaking door he saw that they also sold wool, but after fighting off an impulse to buy several balls of it and some knitting needles, he instead described some coat buttons and the shrewish lady found some that he said were a very good match. He bought three of them, plus a little sewing kit, before moving on to a tiny bank. After using the cashpoint he decided against going inside, as he had no address with which to open an account, so he proceeded to the hardware store, where he saw one of Victor's customers serving behind the long counter.

The shop was surprisingly busy, so he picked up a roll of duct tape and a packet of screws and paid another assistant, before nodding so solemnly to the man who had witnessed his hysterical shouting after the football match that he almost thought he might have dreamt it, or that there really were two of them. Nigel then passed a ladies hairdresser's and wished he could enter – a couple of days ago he would have done – before walking to the end of the street and turning right. On entering a large newsagent's shop which also sold books, stationery and other sundry items, the first thing he saw was the shapely, jean-clad behind of a lady who was bending to arrange some magazines. Even before she straightened up he had seen that she wore no wedding ring, and when he smiled into her dark brown eyes he felt a slight tingling sensation in the back of his head and neck. He took off his cap and put it in the plastic bag from the hardware store.

"Hola," he said to the slim-faced woman who he guessed to be just the right side of thirty for his purposes. She was pretty, but not too pretty, and he estimated her intelligence to be slightly above average; cleverer than Ana, but not remarkably bright.

"Hola," she replied, taking in his wide-eyed, somewhat innocent expression. "What can I get you?"

"Just a newspaper, please," he said, picking up a Periódico de Extremadura and folding it. While she walked around the counter he surveyed the shop with approval, before gazing at her placidly and beginning to take his wallet from his shorts pocket. Just then an old lady dressed in black entered, so he smiled at the young woman and went off to look at the books. When the old lady left he continued to browse for a while, before picking up a thick paperback by Carlos Ruiz Zafón.

"Is this good?" he asked her.

"La Sombra del Viento? Yes, I enjoyed it and it's still very popular," she said in a clear voice that didn't sound altogether uncultured. She smiled too, revealing her fine teeth, and though her lips were a little thinner and her nose a little sharper than he would have liked, he found her face pleasing. She wore a touch of makeup and he was now sure that she couldn't be any younger than thirty-two and maybe as old as thirty-six. She was about five foot six, only an inch or two shorter than him, which ought to help them to see eye to eye.

"I'm still perfecting my Spanish, you see, and I need to read more," he said in his very best Spanish.

"Are you the man who is staying at the hotel?" she asked, which he thought admirably direct.

"Yes, that's me. I'm a writer, in English of course, so you may have heard that I've been asking many questions around the village."

Just then a man entered, and the fact that she attended him quickly seemed to be a promising sign.

"Adiós, Jorge… Yes, I heard that you were planning to build a hotel or something."

Nigel took a deep breath and exhaled slowly, nodding pensively as he did so. Had he not been holding a newspaper in one hand and a book and two bags in the other he would have crossed his fingers.

"I… well, I'm researching a book which will be set in a Spanish village, so I've been asking people all sorts of things and listening to their reactions."

"And saying all sorts of things too, I believe," she said with a note of scepticism that didn't displease him.

"Yes, that too, for the same reason. Before coming here I stayed in a town called La Puebla de Montalbán near Toledo for a few days. Do you know it?"

"I've heard of it."

"Well, I went there and behaved like a typical tourist. I said all the right things and wasn't very inquisitive, so I often ended up answering their questions about me and finding out nothing about them and their way of life. Ha, it was good for my Spanish, but I got very little material for my book."

"I see," she said, looking less sceptical, but glancing at the doorway again, so he decided to wind up the first act.

"So, when I came here I took a very different approach; too different I now think. I may have to move on, in fact, but I'll see how things go over the next few days. Anyway, I've taken up enough of your time, so I'll pay for these and go."

She charged him and put the book and newspaper in a plastic bag. "What about your friends who are coming to make the film? You'll have to be around when they come, won't you?" she asked him as she handed over the bag, raising her eyebrows in what he thought was a rather mocking way.

He smiled and silently cursed himself. "Oh yes, if they decide to come I'll be here. I like it here and hope I feel able to stay."

"Spain is a free country. Tell me if you enjoy the book."

"I will."

Given that the book was about five hundred pages long, he thought her last statement an encouraging sign. The type of shop she worked in was also fortuitous, as one could buy a newspaper every day and also browse the books if necessary. Though his own feelings about her were still uncertain, he was rather glad that she appeared to be reasonably educated, but only time would tell if she might fit in with his plans. Being a thorough man, he called in at the tobacconist's on his way back to the hotel and bought ten small cigars, though he had never smoked, but he bypassed the shop where Ana's friend worked. Ana would have to remain on hold for the time being, until he had decided how to proceed, but he hadn't discounted her yet.

Back in his room he unpacked his things and lay down on the bed, before spending the next half hour reading through his notebook. Yes, he feared that he had been in a disturbed frame of mind when he had arrived at the village, but he would do his best to make amends from now on.

During the next few days Nigel's daily routine followed the same course. He always left the hotel in his walking gear at about half past eight and after coffee and toast in Sara's bar he headed out into the countryside for a couple of hours. His face and limbs were becoming quite tanned, though he always applied sun cream, and he felt that his walk set him up for the rest of the day and helped to dispel any odd thoughts or urges that he had from time to time. He hadn't used the Do Not Disturb sign again and he usually left his notebook open on the little table by the window, as he suspected that neither Ana nor Eusebio could read English, and even if Eusebio was able to make out a few words – he was sure that Ana wouldn't even try, for she was a good girl – there was nothing wayward about his scribblings, unless one read it closely, both on and between the lines.

After his walk he went for his morning paper and always lingered for long enough to apprise the lady of his progress through the book that he found a little too mainstream for his liking, as he preferred to read the great short story writers such as Chekov, Maupassant, Borges and a few of the more modern ones. Still, he managed about a hundred pages a day and planned to ask her name when he finished it, though he deduced that she was already keen for him to take the first step towards putting their relationship on a more personal footing.

He returned to the hotel at about midday and had so far managed to avoid seeing Ana, though he wasn't overly concerned about bumping into her. After a shower and a rest he put on his suit, without a tie, and repaired to Fernando's restaurant for lunch, where Eduardo always served him and never asked him anything. After a gentle stroll through the village he went to Esteban's bar, where he sat at a table and read the newspaper over his third coffee of the day. He was always reserved but polite, and when Esteban's inevitable question finally arrived, he was prepared for it.

"Ah, Neegel, when can we expect to see this German film crew of yours?" he asked, having bided his time for as long as he could. His reputation as a judge of character was on the line, but he was so confident that he would catch the urbane visitor unawares that he had made sure that his father, Bernardo and three more cronies were close at hand.

"Oh, I meant to mention that. The director will be coming later this week to have a look around and meet a few people. I'll have to book a room for him at the hotel. Would you still like them to film some of the conversations here?"

"Oh, I don't mind," he murmured.

"It must be here," said Esteban's father. "Jose Ramón and I don't go elsewhere and we are the people they must interview if they wish to know about the history of the village, such as it is."

"Right, but I don't think he'll do any filming on the first visit. To bring the crew is quite expensive, you see, so he wants to look at the place and talk to people first. We'll come here, of course."

"We will look forward to it," said Bernardo, before looking sharply at him of little faith.

"Yes, you are both invited to lunch," said Esteban with a brave and, it has to be said, respectful smile.

As usual, Nigel returned to the hotel for a short siesta and, as the ball was now rolling, he booked a single room for Thursday and Friday nights, telling Eusebio the purpose of his friend's visit.

"Ah, at last," he said. "We wondered when they would begin."

"Yes, your friend Esteban seemed surprised, I don't know why," Nigel couldn't help saying, as the inconvenient, costly, but necessary visit hadn't been easy to arrange.

When he later dined lightly at Sara's bar he told her about the visit. "We'll come here, of course. I'm sure he'd like to have a chat with you."

"He'll be most welcome," she said, patting her hair. "And I will invite you both to lunch."

"Gracias, Sara."

Nigel wasn't looking forward to Wednesday much, so on Tuesday morning, the Ruiz Zafón book finally finished, he decided to make his next move with the lady newsagent. If things went well it would buoy him up over the next two days, and if not, well, maybe he'd allow his tightened reins to loosen a little and have some fun. Nigel's idea of fun was a singular one, but he knew from recent experience that to maximise one's pleasure it was necessary to toe the line from time to time.

She was busy when he entered the shop dressed in his suit, but no tie, so he looked at the books and chose one by Arturo Pérez-Reverte just as the last customer left.

"You look very smart today," she said, smiling brightly.

"Yes, I have to go into Plasencia to sort out a few things."

"I see. Oh, this morning a customer told me that the German filmmakers were coming soon."

"Ha, so I'm still news in the village!" He chuckled as he gazed into her eyes.

"I know, they're terrible gossips, but they had almost stopped talking about you. Is it true, about the filmmakers?"

"Yes, but only the director is coming, on a preliminary visit. I'm Neegel, by the way. I should have introduced myself before."

"I know your name. I'm Carla," she said, offering her slim hand after a quick glance out of the door.

"Encantado," he said, holding her hand softly for just a second longer than was necessary.

"Igualmente," she replied, not blushing at all. "So what is your business in Plasencia?"

"Oh, just to the bank. I may buy or rent a house in the village and I want to check the state of my finances."

"Hmm, I would rent if I were you. This is a quiet village and you'll get bored here eventually."

"That's what a nice lady in the supermarket said when I asked if I could put something on the noticeboard. I hadn't thought of renting until then."

"No? Have you never rented a property in all the places you've lived?" she asked with a wry smile.

One secondary advantage of his recent writings was that he had been able to refresh his memory regarding all the nonsense he had uttered. Having a Swedish mother and a supposedly deceased German father, but having lived in London, Quebec and Melbourne had made things unnecessarily complicated, but he had already simplified matters in his mind.

"Only for very short periods. My parents met in London and I was born there. My father was a diplomat, so we moved to Melbourne when I was fourteen and to Quebec when I was nineteen, though we kept a small flat in London. My father died two years ago, of cancer, so my mother spends the summers in Quebec and the winters in London. My sister is a midwife in Quebec. She has two children of her own now," he said, not for the first time, though it proved even easier to say it to Carla than into the mirror.

"I'm sorry about your father."

"Yes, me too, but these things happen." He ran a finger along his neck and under his collar, before looking out into the street. "Listen, Carla, would you like to meet up sometime, for a coffee or something?"

"Not here."

"Oh."

"But somewhere else, maybe. As you know, they gossip about everything here in the village. I've been divorced for the last three years and I still feel that people are watching my every move. Some of the more stupid women think I may try to steal their husbands, and as I see everybody here in the shop I must watch my step. So it's difficult, you see." She pursed her lips and nodded. "I sometimes think I should never have come back here. I trained to be a teacher, but I couldn't get a high enough mark in the state exams, so I took over this place from my parents. My father still helps out from time to time."

"Yes, I've seen him."

"Do you have a car?"

"Not at the moment, but I believe a man called Juan sells them."

"Yes, he sometimes has one or two for sale. Listen, let's speak after your filmmaker friend has gone. I'm sure we can arrange to meet for lunch one day, maybe in Plasencia."

Nigel beamed with such delight that it felt almost genuine. "Yes, yes, we could do that. I'll call in on Saturday when it's quiet. How much is the book?"

"It's a present. Do you not want a paper?"

"No thanks, I no longer need to buy one every day. Until Saturday, Carla."

"Sí, adiós, Nigel."

"Nigel?"

"Ha, I speak some English."

"Nigel it is then, to you." He stepped back from the counter and almost collided with Esteban's father. "Sorry, Sr. Almaraz."

"You are dreaming, young man," he said, eyeing him closely through his thick glasses.

Nigel picked up his little blue rucksack from the hotel before boarding the bus for Plasencia. It looked a little incongruous with his suit, but he intended to buy something that he wished no-one to see.

4

"I don't know how that bloody thing works for a start," Stephen Muir said to Nigel as he sat in his host's room at the hotel on Wednesday morning, holding a large video camera.

"It isn't as complicated as it looks. I bought the fanciest one, but it's for amateurs really."

"I thought the camera was going to be enough," Stephen said, pointing to his bulky Nikon on the bed.

"Yes, we can use that too, but I decided to splash out. I want it to be convincing."

"What the hell's this all about anyway?"

Nigel had met Stephen several weeks ago at a cheap hotel in Madrid. A native of Basildon, he had just started studying for a master's degree in the Spanish capital and had yet to find a flat. They had been out for a few drinks on several occasions and he knew rather more about Nigel than the villagers, though he still remained a hazy figure who had spoken of his vague plans to make a new life for himself in Spain. Although Stephen wasn't German, he was blond and Teutonic-looking, which was fortunate as he was the only person Nigel had got to know at all well during his time in Madrid.

"What's it about? It's about you helping me out of a pickle I've got myself into. You know how I said that I wanted to shake things up a bit wherever I decided to go? Well, I got a bit carried away and this is the only way to keep my credibility."

"Sometimes I think you're not quite right in the head, Nigel."

"Yes, I often wonder myself."

"Why did you come to Spain, anyway? It sounds like you were doing fine back in London at that advertising agency."

"The rat race isn't for me, and when I got my inheritance…"

"It won't last forever."

"No, and bribing you to come over won't help, but it had to be done."

"It's not exactly bribery, mate. I told you I was skint and it's only fair that I get to take my time going back to Madrid after whatever it is you're going to put me through."

"I know, and I'm grateful that you've come. How's your German accent?" Nigel asked in a German accent.

"I think I can do it. How does this sound?"

"Fine, but remember you have to do it in Spanish too."

"Christ."

"I'll explain how this thing works in Spanish, so we can practise," he said in Germanic Spanish. "But don't worry, I'll do most of the talking.

"Sehr gut."

"Ah, do you speak it?"

"I've got a GCSE."

"OK, then throw a few words in now and again. Oh, and my village name is Neegel."

"Neegel?"

"Yes, don't forget. Right, once you've switched it on here, you just have to…"

An hour later the two men headed for the least important of the bars in order to try out their act.

"Hola, Victor. This is my German film director friend, Stefan."

"Buenos días, Victor," Stephen said as gutturally as he dared.

"Hola, are you going to film here today?" Victor asked, tucking in his stained white shirt and glancing at the wilting and congealing tapas in the display cabinet.

"Not if you don't want us to," Nigel said. "Stefan just wants to get a feel for the village, though he might want to film a few short conversations."

Stephen brandished the video camera and tried to smile like Oliver Kahn, his favourite goalkeeper, as Nigel had said that he didn't wish to spend much time in a bar that was every bit as dreadful as he had described.

"Can I get you anything?" Victor asked them.

"A cortado for me," said Nigel.

"Un café con leche, bitte, mein Herr," said Stephen.

While Victor turned to operate the only clean thing in the place, Nigel nudged Stephen, who set the camera in motion, upon which a fairly bright light illuminated Victor's greasy hair.

"Here we are in Victor's bar," Nigel began in English. "It is the filthiest hole in Europe and a breeding ground for vermin of every kind." He put his finger to his lips as Stephen's face began to crease. "All the degenerates of the village assemble here every night to indulge in the most heinous sexual practices imaginable. Only last week the owner…" He pointed at Victor who was now goggling at the camera, "…brought in a beribboned sheep which his customers proceeded to ravish on this very bar. Visitors to Extremadura are advised to enter the bar in groups and always wear strong belts." He paused after his solemn discourse. "Cut, I think."

"Wunderbar, Neegel," said Stephen, red in the face but bearing up admirably. "I think we can use that," he added in Spanish.

"You will use it?" Victor asked, aghast.

"Yes, with your permission, of course," said Nigel. "Spontaneous commentaries are best. Replay it for him, Stefan."

As Victor viewed his mute performance on the little screen he began to shake his head. "Oh, no, no, Neegel. I look silly. I wasn't prepared. When you come back please let me know beforehand."

"Very well, we won't use that bit. How about those coffees?"

After leaving Victor in a suitably agitated state, they killed some time by filming and photographing around the village, and Nigel did some pertinent commentaries outside the church, the village hall, the junior school and in the square. He greatly enjoyed his impromptu role, but warned himself not to get carried away. On passing Carla's shop he had merely waved from the street, making sure that Stephen, who was dressed almost as smartly as himself, was clearly visible with his big Nikon over his shoulder and the video camera upon it.

"I wasn't looking forward to this, but it's quite a laugh, isn't it?" Stephen murmured as they approached the hotel.

"Yes, I wasn't sure if you'd like it, so I was a bit worried, but you're playing the part just great, so it's fun for me too. Just give me a frown if you think I ever go too far though. The whole idea of this is to increase my standing, not lower it."

"Will do," said Stephen, delighted that even the potentially onerous part of his all-expenses-paid break was proving to be pleasurable. Nigel's reservations about him were as nothing compared to Stephen's own qualms about his friend's state of mind, as he'd done some odd things back in Madrid. For all he'd known before this morning, the villagers might have been on the point of lynching his strange, stocky friend, as he'd been quite anxious and very insistent on the phone.

"Hola Eusebio," Nigel said to the lounging hotelier, who jumped to his feet and smiled like never before at him and his German film director friend. Eusebio had left his lair four times that morning in order to track the progress of the duo, including a flying visit to Victor's bar, so he had already prepared a few things to say to the camera.

"Hola, Neegel. I am Eusebio, the owner of this modest hotel," he said to Stephen with a little bow.

"Stefan. Encantado," he growled through his Oliver Kahn smile, as Nigel had already told him that Eusebio's silver screen dreams were not going to be fulfilled today.

"We're going to rest for a while now, Eusebio, before having lunch at Esteban's."

"Right," he said, folding his skinny frame into his supremely unergonomic chair. Nigel was sure that Eusebio's posture had worsened since his arrival.

Just then Ana came down the stairs carrying a large laundry bag. On seeing Nigel for the first time in days, she blushed and was about to go on her way.

"Ah, Ana," he exclaimed with delight, as if she were the last person he had expected to see. "Allow me to introduce you to Stefan, my German film director friend."

"Hola," they said to each other.

"Ana is my favourite person in the whole village and has been a great help to me since I arrived here." He looked at the open-mouthed woman. "Would you like to take part in one of our preliminary interviews, Ana?"

"No," she said, before stooping to pick up her sack and making no further eye contact as she hurried through the front door.

"How strange," said Stephen.

"Women," said Eusebio.

"Let's go upstairs," said Nigel.

"What was up with her?" Stephen asked when he had closed the door of his room.

"Hmm, she may feel neglected. I've been avoiding her for a while."

"What for? She's quite a stunner. You could do a lot worse."

"She'd hardly be a great intellectual companion," said Nigel.

"So what? She's obviously got the hots for you, so why not ask her out or something?"

"She doesn't fit in with my plans at the moment."

"What plans? I thought you were going to cast off the shackles of working life and have some fun. I'd have thought you could have a lot of fun with her."

"My idea of fun isn't necessarily the same as other people's."

"Fucking weirdo."

"Yes, well, let's chill out for a while before we embark on the main event of the day; of your stay, in fact."

"I can't wait," he said, slumping onto the bed. "Come back in an hour. I was up at five this morning."

"OK."

When they entered Esteban's bar at twenty two, Nigel wasn't entirely surprised to see about fifteen people, a dozen more than the usual pre-lunch 'crowd'. They were mostly men he had seen in the other bars, plus Eusebio, who was skulking around the corner of the L-shaped bar, nursing a glass of wine.

"I see you are busy today," Nigel said to Esteban after introducing Stefan to him.

"Wednesday's are usually busy," he lied, smoothing down a snow-white apron that Nigel hadn't seen before. He'd had a haircut too, the perpetrator of which was seated next to Bernardo. Roberto's head was freshly shaven and he must have shut up shop early, judging by the empty beer glass and plate of peanut shells before him.

"These people are obviously expecting a show," Stephen said to Nigel in rapid Germanic English.

"Then we will give them one," Nigel replied, a strange gleam in his eyes.

"Sehr gut, but remember not to do anything daft."

"I'm tempted to throw caution to the wind, Stefan," he said with a narrow-eyed smile.

"Suit yourself, but remember how much it's cost you to get me here."

"Money isn't everything. In any case, if you feel up to it, I'd like you to sort of take the lead. You're supposed to be the director, after all, not just the cameraman."

"Who do you want to interview?"

"That fat git behind the bar. Him and only him. Set it up for me, mate."

All eyes were now on the two foreigners who appeared to be having an earnest technical discussion, so when the German handed the Englishman the cameras and clapped his hands, they all sprang to attention on their stools, chairs or feet.

"Guten Tag, first I will film from right to left, so please look natural. Then I will focus on the owner here and my colleague Neegel will ask him a few questions, so carry on talking quietly just as if we weren't here." He scanned the bar, before letting his sharp blue eyes come to rest on Esteban. "Today is just a test, so don't be nervous. Neegel, are you ready?"

"Sí." He handed over the video camera, which Stephen put on his shoulder, and passed the Nikon to Bernardo.

"Gut. Achtung!" Stephen cried, thinking it meant action, before raising his left arm in what looked very much like a fascist salute and bringing it down sharply. Most of the men at the bar looked furtive as Stephen panned the camera past them, and a couple were hunched up on their stools as if they were having a difficult time on the lavatory. Esteban's eyes bulged as the lens came ever nearer, but he managed a smile when the light finally shone on his face.

"Today we are with Esteban, the owner of one of the most popular bars in this vibrant village in Extremadura," said Nigel in Spanish, trying to sound like Andrew Marr in one of his more enthusiastic moments. He had displaced Bernardo from his usual stool in order to get in the shot, and he regretted not having bought a microphone to wave about. "Tell me, Esteban, how has life changed in the village over the last twenty years."

On hearing this, Esteban's father stood up at his table and brandished his stick, but his friend managed to prevent him from blurting out that *he* was the man Nigel should be interviewing, not his hapless son, whose subsequent reply seemed to vindicate what he was almost certainly going to say.

"Er... well... er... there are more cars now, and.... a few more houses," he stuttered, all eyes upon him.

"I see, and would you say that the people have changed? Have the old ways of doing things been lost?" he asked, knowing that his seemingly innocuous question was a tricky one, as very little would have changed since the mid-nineties, and not a tremendous amount in Esteban's fifty or so years of life.

"Yes... no, I mean yes." His harried expression then melted away, and he managed another smile. "Yes, yes, we have a more modern outlook these days. We think that rural tourism will soon come to our historic village. As well as the fine church and other buildings, visitors will find the agriculture interesting too."

"Damn machines!" his father's voice wailed from across the room.

"In this area we breed the finest pigs in Spain and it is delightful to watch them eating the acorns in their natural habitat, as they have done for hundreds, if not thousands of years."

"As well as more accommodation for tourists, do you think there will be more places to eat? Places which might combine traditional dishes with the nouveau cuisine that modern tourists appear to desire?"

"Yes... well, yes and no. I think the current establishments will adapt to the new times and provide everything the tourists desire," Esteban said, looking pleased with his fluent delivery under pressure.

"So, will you be making changes in this very... spartan bar?"

"Er, yes, I will be modernising it soon."

"Will the tourists want modern bars?"

"I will modernise it in a traditional way. I.... I will make it look very old and rustic, like it used to be."

"So will you, for example, change these PVC windows for wooden ones?"

Stephen focused on the dusty window to the left of the bar, with its yellowing frame and rusty iron bars outside, before homing in on Esteban's glowing face.

"Yes, when it is clear that the tourists will come, I will do that, and... other things."

"But won't you have to do that first to attract the tourists? It is, after all, a chicken and egg situation, is it not?" Nigel asked, hoping that the expression existed in Spanish.

"Yes, of course, I..." He looked around the bar for inspiration. "I will soon retile the floor, with traditional terracotta tiles," he said, clearly unhappy with the turn the conversation had taken.

"And perhaps replace those metal chairs and tables with wooden ones? If I were a tourist, I certainly wouldn't like to sit on those ugly things."

"Yes, that too."

At this point both of Stephen's eyes appeared over the camera and gave Nigel a warning look.

Nigel smirked. "Do you have any plans to improve your kitchen facilities, Esteban? At the moment I believe you only offer a limited menu, but when the tourists arrive I'm sure you intend to offer a vast selection of traditional and modern dishes," he said, before turning to give a sniggerer an admonishing look.

"Yes, yes, I will do all these things… soon," he said, his head beginning to drop.

"Thank you for your interesting observations, Esteban," he said, before giving the camera a prolonged smile.

"And cut!" said Stephen. "Wunderbar. Das ist excellent."

The spectators, having entirely failed to keep up a hum of natural conversation, now began to do so. The foreigners' performance had seemed very professional to most of them, but they were as bemused as Esteban regarding the content of the interview.

"That was good, Esteban, thank you," said Nigel quietly.

"But Neegel, that was just a practice, wasn't it?" he replied after downing the glass of beer he had just poured himself.

"Well, yes, but they might be able to use it if the light is all right. Sometimes spontaneous interviews are the best ones."

"But all that about my windows and chairs! Who wants to hear that?"

"These are decisions that all modern hostelries have to take. Besides, German filmmakers like to be innovative. They don't want to hear the usual things about churches, fiestas and suchlike."

"Well, I'd prefer to do the interview again," he said, looking peevish. "And know what the questions are going to be beforehand."

"Ha, that would be cheating! Anyway, how about that lunch you promised us?"

"Hmm, take a seat and I'll be over shortly," he said, before taking payment from his rapidly dispersing customers.

"Come and interview me!" Esteban's father shouted from his domino table.

"Next time, Sr. Almaraz. Today is just a rehearsal."

"My barber's shop is very traditional," said Roberto on passing, though he had been meaning to refurbish it for years.

"Next time, Roberto, I promise."

"I can take you to see some fighting bulls, on the finca where I used to work," said Bernardo.

"That is interesting. Yes, that would be great," said Stephen, having embraced his role so well that for a moment he thought he really might be coming back with a full crew.

The cured ham, garlic soup and fried lamb that Esteban served them was so good that Nigel suspected that it hadn't been prepared on the premises, but the fine meal, washed down with a bottle of Ribera del Guadiana red, resulted in a promise to scrap the interview, but not before he had made Esteban squirm by playing it back to him, twice.

"Ha, look how your mouth falls open here, Esteban," he said to the flushed proprietor.

"Hmm, it's not so easy, but you seemed very relaxed and professional, Neegel."

"Neegel is very modest," said Stephen, also flush after drinking most of the wine. "He has worked with my team before and I have tried to persuade him to take it up professionally."

"Oh, I have other plans," Nigel said with a shrug.

"We are still uncertain what your plans are," said Esteban, looking relieved after Nigel's promise. He still didn't know why he had been put on the spot, but he guessed that the world of show business worked in mysterious ways.

"Well, there are many things to consider. By the way, do you know of a house to rent in the village? I can't stay at the hotel indefinitely, as it isn't cheap."

"I will ask. So, that film, you will erase it?"

"Yes." He switched on the camera and pressed a few buttons. "Now it is gone."

"Gracias, Neegel. Café?"

"No, gracias. We'll take coffee at Fernando's."

"Oh."

"We are lunching at Sara's tomorrow, you see, and we have to go into Plasencia later, so we ought to pay him a short visit, though Stefan isn't interested in filming there."

"Good… I mean OK." He looked at Stefan. "I hope to see you again before you go."

"I expect so, and if not I'll see you in a few months."

"A few months?"

"Yes, I have to schedule the filming and I have a very busy summer programme," he said, as Nigel had requested him to, being keen to prolong the film crew myth for as long as possible.

"Maybe your bar will look a little different when Stefan returns, Esteban?"

"What? Oh, yes, I expect so," he said with a strained smile.

"We will do almost all of the filming in the most traditional bar in the village, I think," said Stephen, getting into the spirt of things, or Nigel's spirit of things. "The film will be seen throughout Europe."

"When Stefan returns with his team, they will do most of the filming in the most traditional bar in the village," Nigel said to Fernando half an hour later.

"The film will be seen throughout Europe," Stephen added.

"Well, my restaurant is the most traditional, as you can see."

"At the moment, yes," said Nigel, moving his head from side to side in the Spanish way. "How much are the coffees?"

"I invite you. Are you sure you won't come to dinner?"

"No, sorry, we have to go into Plasencia to do some more preliminary filming."

They didn't *have* to go into Plasencia, but Nigel thought they deserved a break and he wanted to treat Stephen to a stress-free, slap-up dinner. Things had gone far better than he had expected and the spontaneous recurrence of the rural tourism theme made him ponder the idea for the first time in a while. Persuading the owners to refurbish their bars would be a mischievous source of pleasure for him, but he couldn't help thinking that there might be more potential in the scheme. What Stephen had said was true – that his inheritance wouldn't last forever – though he was yet to reveal to anyone the true nature and extent of his windfall.

Some time later Nigel drove his friend's hire car along the flat road to Plasencia and Stephen marvelled at the Roman aqueduct, the medieval walls, the huge cathedral and the numerous other old buildings.

"Why didn't you come to live here instead? It's a lovely town," Stephen said as they occupied their table at the Restaurante Succo, just off the Plaza Mayor.

"Yes, it is, but it's too big for my purposes."

"Just what *are* your purposes, Nigel?"

"Oh, you know, to be somewhere where I can get to know practically everybody and then… well, play it by ear."

"Are you still writing?"

"Oh yes."

"What about?"

"Oh, this and that, you know, making notes and jotting down impressions."

"About how you've stirred things up?"

"Ha, yes. If I'd just gone about my business they'd have soon got used to me being around. It's been hit and miss so far, but the film crew idea was a stroke of luck. I just said it off the top of my head when Esteban was quizzing me and it was only later that I thought of you. You've been brilliant and by the time we've finished the whole village will be buzzing with it."

"I know, but what's the point of it, really?"

"What's the point of anything? What was the point of commuting into London every day just to make money doing something pointless?"

"Hmm, maybe my master's degree is a bit pointless too," said Stephen.

"Not at all. It's interesting and it's a means to an end. You just have to make sure that the end is worth all the effort."

They spoke little as they ate their turbot and seafood platters and sipped the Albariño white wine. Only over coffee did Stephen broach the subject of Nigel's aspirations once more. It was true that he seemed to be more in his element in the village than in Madrid, where his daft chat-up lines hadn't impressed the allegedly sophisticated metropolitan girls, but he was still concerned about the future of his curious friend.

"Where do you see yourself three months from now, Nigel?"

"In the village. I'll probably rent a house there and see how things go."

"You could ask Ana out. After we've done, your star will be bright, so you ought to take advantage of that."

"Yes, but women are a strange breed. In that area I want to have fun too, but I don't want to upset anyone needlessly. Ana's a straightforward girl and it's about time she found herself a husband. I wouldn't want to mess up her chances. There's another young lady I'm interested in, a bit older than me, and a lot more savvy than Ana. I think we're going to come here on a date sometime next week."

"Will I be meeting her?"

"I can point her out if you like, but we won't be involving her in this filming nonsense."

"Will you tell her it's nonsense?"

"Oh I don't think so. It'll form part of my persona." He smiled, sipped his coffee and shook his head. "I don't know, I've never been really close to a woman. I mean, I've had short-term girlfriends, but I had a feeling they wanted to tie me down, whereas I've always wanted to escape."

"From what? Where to?"

"That remains to be seen. Have a brandy. I'll drive back."

5

The second day's filming wasn't quite as amusing as the first, but it was just as effective in its way. After breezing past Eusebio with the briefest of greetings, they had a late breakfast at Fernando's restaurant, where the owner himself served them while Eduardo looked on vacuously from a barstool, pleased to be getting a rest for once.

"No, Fernando, we don't need to film here today," Nigel said in response to his offer to face the camera.

"We are sure this is the best place to do our main filming, you see," said Stephen. "I filmed a little at Victor's and Esteban's and will do so at Sara's later, but only to get some background material. Esteban knows that his bar would have to be *much* more traditional to feature in the main film, and we will tell Sara the same thing."

"What about Victor's?" Fernando asked with a leer. He was an ugly man and his hawkish eyes were the main feature of his otherwise flaccid face.

"Oh, Victor would have to do a lot of work to his bar in order to have a chance of appearing in the documentary," said Nigel in a solemn voice. "Still, they all have time to make improvements, as Stefan won't return with his team until October at the earliest."

"I have a busy summer," Stephen said. "First to Norway and then to Sweden. We must film there while the weather is good."

Fernando offered them coffee when they had finished their bocadillos of the finest jamón ibérico that he stocked.

"Thank you, but we'll take coffee with Esteban. Yesterday he spoke about refurbishing his bar and Stefan has a few suggestions to make to him." Nigel looked around the wood-panelled dining room. "Would you say this is traditional enough, Stefan?"

"Yes… I think so." He stood up and took a few quick photos. "It is perhaps a little too… perfect, but it is the best place in the village right now."

On this mischievous note, they thanked Fernando for the free grub and strolled over to Esteban's, where Stefan told him that as long as he changed the door, windows, floor, paintwork, tables and chairs, at least a quarter of the hour-long documentary would be filmed there.

"Should we say the same to Victor?" Stephen asked when they had left the pensive proprietor to consider his future.

"No, I think we'll let the grapevine take care of him. Besides, I doubt he's got the cash to do that hole up."

"Why are you staring into space like an imbecile?" Esteban's father asked his goggle-eyed son.

"It would cost a fortune." He looked around his bar. "And there is nothing wrong with it."

"But the tourists won't come here to see a bar like thousands of others."

"What tourists, Papá? There are just a few in summer."

"They will come," said the old man with great sagacity. "They will come and you won't be prepared. Anyway, this is still technically my bar, so you will do as the German suggested. I can't take my money to the grave after all, can I?"

"No, Papá," he said, though his wife had been planning a world cruise to commemorate her father-in-law's passing.

"Will you call the builders, or shall I?"

"I'll do it, Papá, soon."

"Today."

"You seem to have more respect for women than for men," Stephen said as they left Sara's bar that afternoon, having eaten several exquisite tapas and sampled her light and delicious Extremaduran pastries.

"Maybe you're right. When I started the interview I just didn't feel like putting her on the spot. She came across quite well, didn't she?"

"Yes, and the bar doesn't need all that much doing to it. It's in a good place too, on the main road. God, I'm starting to believe that I really am going to come back with my film crew!"

"Ha, yes, I get that feeling too. We must be good actors. I tell you what though, the more I harp on about rural tourism, the more I think it could really happen. It's a pretty village, the countryside's nice, and it's not too far to the mountains."

"Or to Plasencia. Maybe you should look into it seriously."

"I haven't got the capital." He straightened the lapels of the suit that would soon need dry-cleaning. "Let's just walk past the village hall though. I haven't met the mayor yet and he might be there."

The large, hefty wooden door to the white, two-storey building was ajar, so Nigel tapped on it and stepped inside. He heard a rustling sound in a room to the left, so he cleared his throat.

"Con permiso," he called.

"Come in!" A large man in his fifties popped his head round the door and smiled. He had long, grey, receding hair and a bushy grey beard and moustache. Not satisfied with this hairiness however, he also appeared to have cultivated his nostril hairs and his ears were of an exquisite furriness. Dressed as he was in dusty blue overalls, he was clearly not a man to whom elegance meant much.

"Are you the mayor?" Nigel asked, because despite his appearance he had an authoritative air, and was carrying a folder.

"Yes, Enrique Gómez at your service," he said in a clear, deep voice, before holding out a huge, calloused hand.

"Neegel Hamson. I'm staying at the hotel. This is my friend Stefan who has come to visit me."

Enrique nodded and gave both their hands a good squeeze, before leading them into what looked like the council chamber. "I have heard about you. I believe you are filming around the village," he said, showing none of the usual signs of wanting to be filmed, like patting his hair or gazing at the cameras that Stephen carried.

"Yes, I'd hoped to meet you earlier, but this place is usually closed and I haven't seen you in the bars," said Nigel, liking the look of this cheerful, open-faced man.

"I have little time to spend in the bars right now. I work away from here, you see. I've just come to pick up some documents that I have to study this weekend, but please take a seat for a moment." He pointed to two blue office chairs at the end of a long table and sat down on a third. "So, what is this documentary about?" he asked Stephen, who looked at Nigel.

"About village life in Spain. At the moment we're just trying to ensure that this is the best place to film. We're speaking to people and filming a little, to see who might come across well."

"If I get the approval of my bosses, I will return in the autumn with a film crew. We would like to interview you, of course," Stephen said in the slightly German accent that was now second nature to him in Spanish.

The mayor gazed at the two men and smiled. "I take it you won't be filming with that?" he asked, pointing to the video camera.

Nigel thought quickly. "Oh, no. That's just a camera that Stefan has given me."

"In appreciation of him finding this delightful village."

"We've been using it to test people's reactions to being filmed," said Nigel.

"And I will show the footage and the photos I've taken to my bosses, of course," said Stephen, thinking what a fine double-act they had become after a day and a half.

"Well, when you come back in the autumn we can arrange an interview," said Enrique. "Ha, I will wear decent clothes and sit over there." He pointed to a large, padded chair at the head of the table. "And apart from the filming, why else are you here, Nigel?"

Nigel absorbed the correct enunciation of his name without flinching. This Neegel business would have to end sooner or later and he would claim that he had been too polite to correct the mispronunciation, or that Nigel was hard for Spaniards to say, or both.

"Well, I'm looking for a quiet life," he said, wondering how much this perceptive man knew about his antics. "I've been under some stress lately and not feeling quite well, so I left London and went to Madrid. That was no good for me, so I got on a bus and headed west, and here I am." He lifted his hands and let them drop onto his thighs.

"And are you feeling better now?" Enrique asked, gazing solemnly into Nigel's eyes.

"Yes, I'm slowly beginning to feel like myself again. Working with Stefan has helped, though I'm really trying to become a writer."

"To become a writer?"

"Yes, but I have yet to publish anything."

"I see. It's just that my niece Carla told me that you *were* a writer, so I assumed you were already established in the trade."

"Ah, Carla, yes. Well, we just had a quick chat in the shop and there was no time to elaborate." He tried to look self-effacing and hoped the mayor hadn't noticed his almost audible gulp.

"Well, we always try to impress the ladies, don't we?"

"Yes, I guess we do."

"I also heard that you were interested in developing rural tourism in the area."

"Yes, well, I think it would work, but I'm not in a position to promote it myself," Nigel said, beginning to feel like one of his interview victims.

"No?"

"No, I'm afraid my enthusiasm got the better of me and I exaggerated a little at first. I still felt a bit insecure and… not quite right, but I've tried to put that straight."

"And your Spanish is now very good all the time?"

"Ha, yes, that was another silly thing I did."

"Why?"

"Why?"

"Yes, why?"

"Oh, to attract attention, I suppose."

"Nigel is much better now," Stephen interposed. "When I knew him in Madrid he was still feeling very insecure, but when I arrived yesterday I saw that he was much better."

"Good, I'm glad," Enrique said, opening the folder on his knee. "I must go home now, but here is my card." He handed one to Nigel. "I am also interested in rural tourism and I believe the subject of your filming is generating a lot of interest in it. I wish to take advantage of this dynamism among the usually… inert villagers and see if we can finally start to promote it seriously.

Other villages around Plasencia have already begun and we are lagging behind. Please call me on my mobile phone if you want to talk about it some more, Nigel."

"I will… Enrique. Thanks for your time."

"Not at all. Have you finished filming now?"

"We just have to carry out an interview with Eusebio."

"Of course, the only hotel in the village will be of interest to the viewers." He looked at Stephen. "If the documentary is finally made."

"Do you think he's rumbled us?" Stephen asked Nigel as they headed back to the square.

"I don't know, but he's bloody sharp for a guy who looks like he's just left Woodstock. I wonder why he's a digger driver. I'm sure he's educated."

"Yes, maybe he dropped out of whatever he was doing, like you."

"Hmm, could be, but he's come back home. I wouldn't want to do that."

"Make this place your home then, but you'd better be straight with him."

"I've already started, and the woman I mentioned to you yesterday, that's his niece."

"Hmm, go easy then. Am I going to see her?"

"I'd rather you didn't. Another time maybe. Let's go and grant Eusebio his greatest wish. The mayor seems to find out everything and we've only done one serious interview so far. I hope Esteban doesn't go telling him that we've tried to bully him into doing up his bar."

"That's not like you, Nigel," said Stephen, patting him on the shoulder.

"What isn't?"

"To worry so much about what someone thinks of you."

"No, I know, but he's just about the only serious person I've met here, or the only serious man, as Sara's all right," he said, thinking of Carla. "I feel a certain respect for him, despite his hairiness."

"Yes, I'd love to get at those nostrils with a pair of shears."

"Ha, but that's it, you see. He couldn't give a toss about things like that. The people I was supposed to respect, like my bosses back in London, were mostly complete phoneys who only cared about making money."

As they were near a bench in the square, Stephen sat down and Nigel followed suit. "What about your family?"

"My dad died."

"Yes, you told me."

"I told you a lot of lies about my family. I'm afraid."

"Oh."

"My dad did die, of cancer. I wouldn't joke about that. What did I tell you he did?"

"That he was a roving photographic journalist."

"And I told Carla he was a diplomat. Did I tell you we lived in Quebec and Melbourne?"

"London, Quebec and Sydney, but you were drunk at the time."

"We lived in Harlow, and still have a place there."

"That's not far from me. I thought your accent was pretty similar to mine, though a bit posher."

"My dad was a GP. My mum's a teacher, but his life insurance was so good that she's retired early. My sister's in Quebec, married to a Canadian, so she spends the summers there with her grandkids."

"Your sister the midwife?"

"Yes, that's right. I've spent quite a bit of time there over the years."

"That just leaves Australia then."

"I spent a couple of months there before going to university, so I know enough about it."

"What was the point of lying about them?"

"Oh, just another way to escape. I mean, bloody hell, I studied marketing in Leicester and then went to work in London. It's not exactly the stuff that dreams are made of. London kills people like me. It's an open sewer of superficiality."

"You should write that down."

"I already have. Anyway, that's the real me."

"And did you really get an inheritance, or are you just living off your savings?"

"What did I tell you about that?"

"Nothing much. You just mentioned it a couple of times."

"Let's leave it that way then, unless you want to get me lying again."

"No, no, it's none of my business."

"Anyway, let's maintain this sincere and serious tone and go and interview that oaf Eusebio."

Eusebio received the news of his unexpected interview with some trepidation, as Esteban had already told him that as a result of *his* grilling, his father was going to make him renovate the bar from top to bottom, inside and out. In the event, however, Nigel didn't mention the decor at all, instead asking him a series of easy questions about his clientele, the village, and the surrounding area.

"And cut!" said Stephen for the last time.

Eusebio wiped his forehead with his handkerchief and leant on the reception desk behind which he had remained ramrod straight for ten minutes. "Is that it?"

"Yes, you were very good," said Nigel.

"I thought you would ask me if I planned to make my hotel more rustic for the tourists."

"No, the hotel is fine as it is for now."

"For now?"

"Yes, I mean, to refurbish it all would cost a fortune. You must wait to see if the tourists do arrive in larger numbers before making such a large investment."

"But Esteban has already called the builders. They will give him an estimate tomorrow."

"Oh, that's a few thousand euros and will transform his bar into something much more... palatable."

"You could do one thing, Eusebio," said Stephen.

"What?"

"Change those plastic signs outside for some wooden ones, illuminated by little spotlights. That will make a big difference for relatively little money."

"Hmm, I'll think about it. Gracias."

The following morning Stephen gave Nigel a lift into Plasencia, from where he would wend his way east to Madrid, though he had given some of his expenses money back to Nigel.

"I hope you get on all right," he said.

"Yes, we'll see what develops. I hope your course goes well too. Maybe I'll come to visit you soon."

"To Madrid? But you hate it."

"Yes, but you can hardly come back here, or not for a long time, unless you happen to meet a German film crew who're at a loose end."

"That's true. Keep in touch."

"Yes, I'll email you soon. Drive carefully."

On the straight road across the Spanish plain Stephen reflected that Nigel was in a much better place than he had been a month earlier, both physically and mentally.

On the bus back to the village, after buying a few casual clothes, Nigel thought that if he wasn't careful his life might become a humdrum affair again. "But what can I do?" he murmured to himself. "Just toe the line for a bit, my boy, and see what transpires."

6

After brisk early morning walks, Nigel spent much of the weekend writing, only leaving the hotel for his meals. On Sunday evening Esteban seemed preoccupied, so he asked him why.

"Oh, this building work. I now have two quotes and my father wants the work to commence right away."

"I see." Nigel stirred the cup of tea that he had finally taught him how to make correctly, looked around the bar, and came to a decision. "Listen, Esteban, I'm going to start looking into this rural tourism business seriously. I spoke to Enrique on Friday and I think he'll back me up, so I'm going to do some research and see if we can do anything in time for the summer."

"Enrique? The mayor?"

"Yes."

"Two or three years ago he tried to convince us to try to attract more tourists, but we paid no attention. Now he's very busy in his job – I think he's travelling to Cáceres every day – and he hasn't mentioned it for a while."

"He's still keen, and I've got the time to look into it."

"But it is May now, so a little late for this summer, no? I imagine that after the documentary has been shown all over Europe there will be more interest in our village."

"Yes, but that's by no means certain, you know. Stefan has to sell the idea to his bosses first, and at the moment they seem more interested in Scandinavia. Besides, the film is only one tool among many."

"Like what?"

"That I intend to look into."

On Monday he caught the early bus into Plasencia, bought a cheap laptop computer, returned to the village, and found that there was no Wi-Fi in the hotel.

"Eusebio, there is no Wi-Fi here."

"No, there's no call for it. People can use their fancy phones, can't they?"

"Yes, but not their other devices. People expect Wi-Fi these days, you know. Besides, how am I supposed to use my new laptop to research rural tourism… for you?"

"Can you not get one of those bongle things?"

"A dongle, yes, but they are slow and expensive to use." He looked at the antiquated computer in reception. "So how do you take bookings?"

"They call me, or walk through the door, just like they always have," he said, a note of defiance in his voice.

"I shit myself on the whore," Nigel said, as people do when they wish to express shock, rage or disappointment. Nigel was merely surprised, but remembered that he himself had stumbled upon the hotel.

"What's wrong?"

"Eusebio, what century are we in?"

"The twenty-first, I believe."

"Eusebio," he repeated, wishing to stress that his words were directed at him alone. "For several years now most people have booked hotels online. There are wonderful websites where one can browse all the hotels in the *world*, before reserving a room."

"Ah."

"How the hell do you expect people to find this place?"

"Well, they do. Today a man from Toledo and a couple from Portugal will arrive."

"Whoopee."

"What does that mean?"

"Nothing. Eusebio. Are you busy now?"

He looked at the panel of room keys. "Well, not very busy."

"Good, because we're going to drive into Plasencia. I'm going to buy a dongle for my laptop and we're going to arrange for the internet to be installed here. As soon as it's operative I'll put your hotel on those websites and it will be seen all over the world. Then people will begin to book rooms for the summer, you will see."

"Is it expensive?"

"The increase in custom will soon pay for the whole year," he said, before explaining that when most people browsed hotels they immediately discounted those which didn't offer Wi-Fi in the rooms.

"But what do they need it for?"

"Eusebio, people are *hooked* on the internet. They cannot live without it. The idea of spending just twenty-four hours offline would be like going without food and water."

"Well, I don't know…"

"Either you do as I say, or I leave today."

"But where would you go?"

"I'll leave the village. I'll step out of the Dark Ages and into the light. I'll wash my hands of the lot of you. I'll tell Stefan to tell his bosses that his team won't be able to use the internet in the hotel. Christ, next week they'll be in *Lapland* and they'll have the internet."

"Lapland? Where the reindeers are?"

"Yes."

Eusebio took his car keys from the drawer.

"Fernando, do you have a website?" Nigel asked that evening.

"Oh yes, my nephew made one some time ago."

Nigel pushed away his plate and opened his laptop on the table. "I don't suppose you have Wi-Fi?"

"What's that?"

"I'll tell you another time." He inserted the dongle, waited, and typed in the name of the village and the word 'restaurante'. "I can't find it."

"What?"

"This place."

"Of course not. You need the name of the website."

"Oh, God."

"What's wrong?"

Nigel explained what was wrong and offered to put it right.

"So you'll make a new website that everyone can see, Neegel?"

"Yes, I know a lot about that sort of thing because of the work I used to do."

"How much will it cost?"

"Nothing, or very little. It's easy for me, just like running a restaurant is easy for you," he said, before pointing out that Eusebio's clientele would soon be increasing considerably, and as he had no dining room, the village hostelries would all benefit. He said all this with great conviction because he was confident of success. After spending several years striving to convince the consumer that one brand of toothpaste was better than another, he now felt that he had a blank canvas to work on. The village was an oasis of ignorance in a rapidly modernising region, and it would be a piece of cake to increase their share of tourism from miniscule to moderate.

"Oh, Neegel, don't tell me that I need one of those websites too!" Esteban lamented the following evening.

"No, don't worry about that, just get the work done. Don't forget the wooden sign with little lights for outside," he said, having decided that all the bars and some other establishment were to have them.

"And who will make that for me?"

"Here are three numbers you can ring to get quotes." He handed him a post-it note. "Sara has already ordered hers, from the second one."

"Has she got a website?"

"No. Eusebio and Fernando will soon have good ones, and that will be sufficient to attract people to the village," he said. He was yet to speak to the mayor about his flurry of activity, because he wanted to show him results before offering to improve the wretched village website and the awful Wikipedia entry which some semi-literate odd-bod must have done.

He was so busy during the following week that he didn't call in to see Carla at all, partly to give himself time to think, but mostly to impress her with his altruistic endeavours when he finally saw her. He was polite to Ana when their paths crossed, but had resolved to flirt with her no more. He hoped that when the village became the small but successful tourist destination that it deserved to be, she would have more opportunities to meet people, and maybe get a better job. In the meantime she was to manage the online bookings which Nigel set up as soon as the internet had been installed, thus making herself indispensable to Eusebio, whose computer skills were limited to filling in a spreadsheet which his tax assessor had set up for him, and printing it out once a month.

Only when he had finished Fernando's new website and begun to work on Eusebio's did he call Enrique, the mayor. He told him briefly what he had done so far.

"Splendid, Nigel. You are an asset to the village. Can we meet at the Casa Consistorial on Saturday at ten?"

"Of course."

On Saturday Nigel took along his laptop, but found Enrique seated at a computer in a little office across the hallway from the council chamber.

"Hola, Nigel. I'm looking at Fernando's new website. It's excellent."

"Oh, it's not bad, though I'd like to take some better photos. I'll activate the bookings system next week when I've shown Eduardo how to use it."

"No easy task. The crucial thing, however, is for Eusebio to get more guests. Do you think he will?"

"Yesterday they took their first online booking. A double room for a week in July, booked from Belgium. Eusebio was speechless."

"With delight?"

"Well, at first because he didn't believe it was real, then with delight when I showed him that they'd chosen the option of paying upfront. I seized the moment and persuaded him to get new wooden signs right away."

"Ha, and Esteban has now closed for refurbishment."

"Yes, he'll reopen in a month."

"We hope. This is Extremadura, remember. Not just Spain, but Extremadura."

"Hmm, but I... well, I helped him to draw up a little contract for the work. If they don't finish in a month, they lose 20%."

"Is old Benjamín doing the work?" he asked, referring to a builder who spent his evenings in Victor's bar.

"No, a company from Plasencia. His quote was too high and he wouldn't have been fast enough anyway."

"He won't be happy."

"I'll make sure he gets some work soon. Sara wants to renovate her bathrooms."

"You have become very dynamic, Nigel."

"Oh, it's nothing compared to how I used to work, and at least I don't have to spend an hour and a half getting home anymore," he said with a chuckle.

"But it is work, nonetheless. I hope they are showing their appreciation." He intertwined his fingers and rested his hands on the table, smiling serenely at Nigel through his abundant moustache.

"Yes, too much. Fernando won't let me pay for anything in the restaurant and Eusebio's given me a big discount."

"You haven't mentioned Victor and his insalubrious tavern."

"No, well, I guess he hasn't got much spare money."

"What? But he makes more than any of them, compared to his costs, at least."

"Really?"

"Yes, his customers *consume*, you see, and I know for a fact that his football channels are pirated. He is a walking goldmine, that man, but a miser."

"Well, hopefully he'll follow suit when he sees what the others are doing."

"If only, but don't worry, I'll have a word with him and persuade him to smarten the place up a bit. We can't have a blot on our little village landscape, can we?"

Nigel was touched by this suggestion that he was no longer a complete outsider. "Would you like me to smarten up the village website?"

"Ah, I've been meaning to do so for some time, but I'm no expert and have little time. Yes, you do it, Nigel, and I will pay you, or the village will pay you."

"No."

"No?"

"No, I don't want to receive any kind of official payment," he said adamantly.

"Why not? Your work is invaluable."

"I'm not doing it for the money, but I do need to find a house to rent. Even with my discount the hotel's still too expensive to stay at long term."

"Then I will find you a house."

"Thanks."

"*And* pay you for your work, because I would also like you to design a tourist brochure for us, and maybe there are more things you can do. A village girl was going to work here on that sort of thing, but she decided to go away to study instead, something I encouraged her to do."

"Did you study anything, Enrique?"

"I am a chemist; an industrial chemist, but I was never happy living far away from here."

"Right. Anyway, I don't want to receive any kind of official payments because I don't want to feel trapped again."

"Trapped?"

"Yes, for me a salary is synonymous with slavery. I know it sounds silly, but I've got plenty of money at the moment and I'm not sure how long I'll be here."

"But you wish to rent a house?"

"Yes, maybe for six months."

"I will look into it and call you."

"Thanks. Oh, who did the Wikipedia entry? It isn't very good."

"Isn't it?"

"No, it's very short and not very well-written."

"I know the culprit well. I will speak to her."

"Would you like me to improve it?"

"No, she must do it."

"Right, fair enough."

"She is my daughter, you see."

"Oh."

"But she was twelve when she did it. She is fifteen now, so I dare say she can improve it."

"Great, I'll leave it to her then."

"I thought you'd stopped reading the papers," Carla said when Nigel finally called in at the shop. She looked cheerful and not at all put out by his long absence. She had her long hair tied back, as usual, and he thought she looked rather like the type of librarian normally only seen in films.

"I have, just about. I've been very busy, you see."

"I know. I get constant updates regarding your humanitarian work."

"Ha, very good. Would you like to see more tourists here?"

"Why not? They'll buy newspapers and the ones who already come are usually nice people; people who like to explore and discover new areas."

Nigel had been having second thoughts about asking Carla out for a date, as although he found her quite attractive, he preferred to remain friends. Knowing the village by now, he suspected that even being seen drinking a coffee together would be misconstrued, so if they were spotted driving off to Plasencia the gossip-mongers would be merciless, and he assumed that she, like Ana, was probably on the lookout for Mr Right.

"Well, I'll get back," he said. "I'm working on the village website now."

"Ah, good. So, when are we going to go out for the day?"

"Er, whenever you like."

"How about this Sunday? My father usually opens the shop for a while in the morning, so I'm free all day. Do you fancy going for a drive and having lunch somewhere?"

"I... well, yes, I'd like that," he said, feeling like a shy teenager again. Even when still in his mischievous mood, he'd had no desire to compromise her, so now that he was on the straight and narrow, for the time being, he felt even less inclined to put the village cats among the pigeons.

"I don't mean on a date, you know," she said to his further bewilderment, though a look of relief soon followed his puzzled expression.

"No, no, not a date."

"But we're grownups, aren't we?"

"Er, yes."

"I'll show you around a bit, so you'll know what else your tourists will be seeing. How about if I pick you up at the hotel at about ten?"

"At the hotel?"

"Yes, or would you prefer to climb into the car boot in the dead of night?"

"No, *I* don't mind you picking me up," he said, imagining Eusebio's leering face, with maybe a few suggestive winks thrown in for good measure.

"At ten then. Do you know Extremadura at all?"

"Not really. I came to Plasencia on the bus from Toledo, and then jumped on the first local bus I saw."

"Lucky you. Until Sunday then."

"Sí, hasta el domingo, Carla."

7

By Saturday both the hotel and village websites were up and running. Fernando's had been easy, as Nigel had merely improved it, but he had emailed his drafts of these last two to Enrique, who had revised them significantly, adding numerous flowery phrases that the Spanish love so much, but which Nigel had toned down for the English version. He had also made a start on a leaflet extolling the virtues of the village, but soon saw that Enrique would have to help him out, and maybe Carla too.

"Yes, I'll have a look at it," she said as they drove south on the mostly flat and extremely quiet dual-carriageway towards Cáceres.

"There's so much *space* here," he said, marvelling at the endless views and lack of traffic.

"Yes, we certainly have plenty of that. I'll turn off here and show you something."

After driving along for a few miles, the road passed over a reservoir which stretched away to the west.

"Good heavens. It's huge!"

"Yes, it's called the José María de Oriol Reservoir. It goes on for over thirty kilometres that way and there's an enormous dam at Alcántara. It's the second largest reservoir in Europe and regulates the flow of the Tagus, the longest river on the peninsula."

"Wow. You know, I think you should be writing the leaflet, not me."

"We'll do it together, if you like."

"Yes, I would."

"Better still, we'll do one for the village and another about the places of interest that can be reached from there. Does Eusebio have any leaflets at the hotel?"

"A few dusty ones. I saw some for a bullfight in Plasencia about five years ago."

"Oh, he's hopeless. We'll write to the tourism department and get them to send us some. Who knows, maybe one day we'll have a tourist office like other villages."

"Nearby villages?"

"One or two, but most of the tourism is in and around the triangle of Cáceres, Trujillo and Mérida."

"I don't know any of those places."

"Today you'll see Cáceres and Trujillo. Mérida is further south and has a wonderful bridge and other Roman remains, but it's a long way from the village. Today's route is one that Eusebio could propose to his summer guests, if he decides to be a little more dynamic."

"He's quite old, isn't he?"

"Sixty-three, I think, the same age as my father."

"Has he no children to take over the business?"

"One son, but he works for the Sabadell Bank in Barcelona. He has a very well-paid job and isn't interested in the hotel."

"A company man. I tried that, but it wasn't for me."

"No, I wouldn't like to live in a big city either."

"It's not just that. It's a way of life in which you must always behave and..." He wondered how to say 'toe the line'. "Well, conform to the expectations of others."

"And could you not do that?"

"For a while, yes, but the problem is that when you see a problem you cannot speak out. You might offend your boss if you appear to undermine him or her. There's a lot of politics involved, with everybody always scheming."

"A microcosm of the world, perhaps."

"Exactly, but out in the world one can choose one's own path."

"And where is yours heading, Nigel?"

"I don't know, but not to two or three more decades of conformity. Is this Cáceres?" he asked as they drove along a road lined with very untouristy factories.

"Yes, it's a big place now. Close your eyes until we reach the city centre."

He didn't, but it wasn't long before she parked on a side street and they walked to the main square.

"This is wonderful, Carla," he said as he surveyed the large car-free plaza surrounded by elegant buildings, some very old and other less so. "What's that?" he asked, pointing to what looked like a miniature castle.

"That's the Bujaco Tower, built by the Moors in the twelfth century upon Roman foundations. We'll walk under that arch and up to the medieval town."

"Well, the village has nothing to match this," Nigel said when they had climbed the cobbled street and toured the churches and palaces. So much old stone all in one place!"

"Yes, it's a world heritage site. The walls are still mainly Arabic, but many of the buildings were constructed with the silver that our conquistadors stole from America."

"Did they come from Extremadura?"

"Most of them, yes. Cortés, Pizarro, Vasco Núñez de Balboa, and a few more. I guess there wasn't much going on here at the time, so they decided to seek their fortunes elsewhere."

"And all this just an hour from the village."

"If you like this, you'll love Trujillo."

"This is even more marvellous, Carla," he said as they stood looking at the castle of Trujillo from the old town an hour later.

"Yes, and as the town hasn't grown so much, it's more atmospheric, I think."

"Is it as old as Cáceres?"

"The castle is, and the original walls, and Pizarro and his brothers came from here, so they built like mad when they came back with the loot."

"Did he have that crazy statue built for himself?" he asked, referring to a mounted knight in the centre of the square who wore a helmet with very strange, receding horns.

"Ha, no, that was built by an American in the 1920s and exhibited in Paris before they brought it here."

"That explains it. How far are we from the village now?"

"Oh, not much over an hour. Our tourists will be able to visit both places in a day easily. We're rushing a little because I want to show you something else after this."

"I can't wait. Let's go and get some lunch, shall we?"

They ate a light lunch which Nigel insisted on paying for, before leaving the town and heading north. During the hour's drive along a quiet dual-carriageway, Nigel was delighted to observe scores of cows, bulls and pigs, before he saw a familiar sight up ahead.

"Isn't that Plasencia?"

"Yes, we have to drive past it, but we're not going far."

After skirting the town they began to climb, imperceptibly at first, but the road soon began to meander up into more wooded terrain and Nigel saw mountains up ahead.

"I've seen those from afar, on my walks, but it's like driving into another country."

"Yes, that's the Sierra de Gredos up ahead. We might still see a bit of snow."

"Really?"

"Yes they're very high; up to 2500 metres, I think. There's even a ski station, but it can only be approached from the north, so it's a long way from the village. Let's stop here and have a look around."

Carla pulled off the road in a place called Jerte and they walked to the northern edge of the village.

"I've seen a hotel and a hostel already," Nigel said.

"Yes, and there are at least three more places to stay in the village, plus a few rural houses nearby. They already have a good tourist trade, and the villages up ahead are even more prepared. This area's popular for walking, cycling and horse-riding."

"Is this still Extremadura?"

"Yes, but we're right on the edge now. Castilla y León begins a few kilometres up the road. Let's find a place to have a drink."

After exploring the village, Nigel concluded that it was nothing to write home about. "Your village has a much nicer church, a better square, and more old houses than this place."

"Yes, but it's greener and hillier up here."

"I still think we can rival places like this. They're closer to the mountains, but let's face it, the majority of tourists drive and stroll rather than hike. We're nearer to the lovely places you've taken me to today, and our bars are soon going to be more rustic than this one," he said, looking at the grey-tiled floor with disapproval.

"Ha, you like that word?"

"Rústico?"

"Yes."

"Well, we British people know a thing or two about attracting tourists. It's attention to detail that counts in the long run."

"Including wooden signs."

"Oh yes, they are indispensable."

"Your Spanish is getting better all the time. Where did you learn it?"

"I taught myself mostly, and spent a lot of time in the tapas bars in London, or the ones run by Spaniards. I already knew French, so it wasn't too difficult."

"Why did you speak it badly some of the time after you arrived?"

"Oh, just being silly, I suppose. I wanted to give myself a jolt and I thought that being eccentric might help. Do you think some people still think me a bit odd?"

"They don't say so, not now."

"But before?"

"Oh, I think your performance in Victor's bar was your main aberration, but they imagined you were drunk, like most of the other men there. Don't worry about it," she said, patting his hand in what he thought was a sisterly way. During the day he hadn't thought about Carla as anything other than a friend, and on the whole he was pleased that she seemed to feel the same way.

Their whistle-stop tour was giving him much food for thought, and he was now sure that he wanted to stay on in the village for at least a few more months.

He sipped his beer. "Enrique's going to try to find a house for me to rent."

"Right, I'll ask around too, if you like."

"Thanks. I only want a six month contract really, so it'll have to be furnished."

"Oh, it will be. People don't generally rent their houses."

"No? Why not?"

"Well, mainly because there's no-one to rent them to, but I know there are a few that have been empty for a while."

"I'd like a sort of casual contract really. You know, I don't really want to be bothered with getting residence papers and all that."

"All what?"

"Well, just that, I suppose."

"Why? Will they make you feel tied down?" she asked with a chuckle.

"Ha, no, but I just don't like the idea of permanence right now, and I am a European, after all. Oh, I suppose I'll get them if I have to," he said, thinking about his financial affairs.

"I don't think it'll matter for the house. I'm sure they'll prefer to be paid in cash, so an informal contract will be best for them too. Come on, we'd better get back."

In a little over forty minutes they were outside the hotel, and after bestowing two kisses and many thanks on his comrade-in-arms, Nigel walked quietly past the reception desk.

"Ah, Neegel, there you are," said Eusebio, appearing over the counter holding a filthy wet rag. "I'm cleaning these cupboards and compartments ready for when all your fellow guests arrive. We've had two more bookings for the summer. It's amazing how people plan ahead."

"Yes, isn't it? Listen, Eusebio, I won't be staying here for much longer, you know."

"No?" His eyebrows rose and his mouth fell open, revealing the gummy part of his upper dentures.

"In spite of your generous discount, it's still too much to pay long term."

"Then we can–"

Nigel raised his hand. "*And* this summer all your rooms will be full. No, I have to find a house to rent."

"Well why didn't you say so?"

"Er, well, I didn't think you'd be too pleased, especially after lowering the price of my room."

"I have the perfect house for you, Neegel," he said, flinging the rag into the small bathroom beyond the reception area.

"Really? Is it yours?"

"Almost. It's my brother-in-law's."

"Does he not use it?"

"Not for a while. He died last winter."

"I'm sorry."

"I'm not. He was an unpleasant man and won't be missed. My wife and her other brother are still deciding what to do with it, but it has hardly been touched since he left it for the final time."

"For the hospital?"

"No, for the mortuary. He died in bed, a nice divan bed which he had just bought, so your mattress will be excellent."

"Was he ill for a long time?" Nigel asked, envisaging the man agonising, sweating and maybe worse.

"No, it was boom!" he said with a loud clap. "Heart attack. My sister called round in the morning and he was lying there stone cold, staring at the ceiling. Perhaps his last thoughts were of the lottery ticket he still owed me for." He shrugged and sighed. "So, the house is vacant and I'm sure I can arrange a cheap rent for you."

"I don't really want a long-term contract, you know. I'd prefer to pay cash, maybe six months up front."

"Nonsense, you can pay every month and leave whenever you like. You'll be doing us a favour."

"I suppose it will need cleaning."

"It will be dusty now, but I'll ask Ana to clean it. She's always keen to work more hours."

"She will, this summer. Well, I'd certainly like to have a look at it."

"Tomorrow morning we can go, Neegel."

"Right." Nigel decided that the time had come, and thought Eusebio the best person to disseminate his startling news. "You know how you call me Neegel, Eusebio?"

"Yes, Neegel."

"Well, that's not quite how it's pronounced... in my own country."

"No?"

"No, it's Nigel."

"Nai-gel?"

"Yes, that's perfect."

"Oof, it will take some getting used to. I always think of you as Neegel, as does everybody else. So why...?"

"Oh, I think someone said it, I can't remember who, and I didn't bother to correct them. Then later on I felt embarrassed to," he said, trying his best to look sheepish and not laugh.

"Nigel. Nigel, Nigel... Nigel. Yes, I like it. Neegel sounded a little German or something, like your friend Stefan."

"Would you mind mentioning it, if you see anyone and my name crops up?"

"Of course... Nigel."

Nigel walked up to his room feeling confident that within twenty-four hours his new name would be widely known.

"So is this where he died?" Nigel asked as he prodded the mattress the following morning.

"Yes, one day he was a grumbling fool, the next he was a peaceful corpse," said Eusebio, grinning as he crossed himself. "They are four days."

"What are?"

"Life, it is short. Don't worry about the mattress. I don't think he's left an impression like the Turin Shroud, and we can turn it over anyway. My sister removed all his clothes and personal belongings this morning."

By then Nigel had toured the small two-storey house near the northern edge of the village and he liked it, apart from the religious paintings and many ugly ornaments that Eusebio promised to remove. The avocado bathroom suite didn't bother him, and he reflected that the good thing about Spanish houses was that the lack of wallpaper and carpets meant that there was far less space upon which the prevalent fashion could be imposed. The lampshades were horrendous, frosted glass affairs, but he could either ignore them or buy some cheap ones in Plasencia. There were two decent sized bedrooms, so if the brother-in-law's ghost bothered him he could move the deathbed into the other one, or if the deathbed bothered him, he could buy a new mattress for one of the single beds in the other room, as he had no plans to cohabit with anyone.

"What do you think, Nai-gel?" Eusebio asked with a leer, making a meal out of his new name. Overnight he had recalled that Nigel had expressly told him that Neegel was the correct pronunciation, so he would probably punish his impudence for some time to come, but Nigel would take it on the chin as long as his real name got around the village without too much fuss.

"I like it. How much a month?"

"How much do you want to pay?"

"Er, ten euros?"

"Ha, your English humour is very funny, Nai-gel." He chuckled, before quickly assuming a more business-like expression. "How about three hundred?"

"Done." He held out his hand, which Eusebio squeezed with his bony fingers. "I can clean it myself though. It's not dirty, just dusty."

"Nonsense, that is woman's work, and Ana will be arriving any minute."

"I think she's capable of more than just cleaning and changing beds, you know. How is she getting on with the bookings?"

"Fine."

"Why not make her receptionist this summer and find someone else to do the cleaning?"

"Then what will I do?"

"Spend a little more time at home."

"What will I do there?"

"Count the money you're going to make."

"If only! There is the internet to pay, and the wooden signs and the spotlights." He shook his head despondently.

"The booking's you've had so far, which you would *never* have got, will pay for those things."

"Ha, I know." He slapped Nigel on the back. "Young man, never admit that you are making money. It's a fatal mistake."

"I'll bear it in mind. I'll stick around and give Ana a hand."

"As you wish, but behave yourselves, eh?"

8

The first thing that Nigel did when Eusebio had left was to open all the windows and let the warm morning breeze refresh the rooms. He then put most of the pictures and ornaments in the wardrobe in the spare room and had just begun to attack the cobwebs when Ana arrived.

"Con permiso," she said as she tapped on the open front door.

"Ah, Ana, please come in. I told Eusebio I'd clean the place myself, you know."

"Men don't know how to clean," she said flatly, before a timid smile dispelled the anxious look on her face. She really was lovely, Nigel thought, and seemed to think it not quite *comme il faut* to be alone in the house with a man.

"I'm getting rid of the cobwebs. I think the place just needs a good dusting. They cleaned it thoroughly after the man… left."

"Ha, a little dusting," she murmured, before entering the kitchen and pulling an array of cleaning products from the cupboard under the sink. "I'll clean the windows first."

"Are they dirty?"

She moved over to the kitchen window and drew her finger from top to bottom, before pointing out the line.

"Right, I'll get on with the cobwebs."

As Nigel moved from room to room toting his broom, the image of Ana with her white apron over her t-shirt and jeans remained lodged in his mind. She had a great figure, a pretty face and lovely dark hair, so what did it matter if she wasn't an intellectual giant? In theory, Carla was more his cup of tea – and only two years older than him, it turned out – so why didn't the memory of her more refined face and less curvaceous but equally appealing figure have the same effect on him? Chemistry, he surmised, but he warned himself to leave Ana alone. For one thing, he suspected that she was a virgin and that a quick roll in the hay, or on the deathbed, wasn't at all what she had in mind, though she might eventually acquiesce as a means to an end. No, he would offer her the same brotherly, or cousinly, friendship as he had Carla and thus avoid any possibility of entrapment. Not that anyone would find it easy to prod him to the altar with a shotgun in his back, as he had no intention of accumulating any more luggage, though he would already have to leave a few things behind if he were forced to do a runner for any reason.

What a way to think! he thought as he reached up into a corner with his broom. Shouldn't he now be flitting from town to town, deflowering every bit of totty who crossed his path, rather than selflessly striving to put this one insignificant place on the tourist map? He knew that wasn't him, however, as he had never been an aficionado of one-night stands, which he thought sordid and unhygienic, but he would still keep his distance from Ana.

"I'll do this window now," Ana said as she stood in the doorway with her little bucket.

"Right, I've done in here," he said, stepping off the deathbed and collecting his harvest of cobwebs. "I've done the other rooms. What shall I do now?"

"Do you really like cleaning?" she asked, seeming unfazed to be in the same room as him, which didn't feel at all like standing in a small hotel bedroom with the door wide open. Here they were far from prying eyes and it struck Nigel that it was brave of her not to have dismissed him from the house on her arrival. At that very moment they could have been defiling the very mattress upon which a denizen of the village had passed away only five month earlier, for all the passing villager knew.

"I don't *like* it, but I've always done my own cleaning."

"Well, help me to take these curtains down. They all need washing."

Nigel looked at the shiny, peach-coloured drapes. "I don't think I'll put them back up. There are blinds too, after all," he said, before beginning to unhook them.

Ana couldn't quite reach the other one, being a mere five foot three or thereabouts, so when he released the last hook she reached up and across to take the curtain, brushing against him as she moved, not with her breast, God forbid, but with her lovely plump forearm. Nigel felt a tingle in his own arm, and stepped aside before the tingle reached his loins.

"Go on, take the other one down," she said.

"Ah, yes," he said, and did so.

Another brush, another tingle, so the first one hadn't been due to clumsiness after all.

"Thanks. Why don't you take the rest of the curtains down while I do this window?" she asked, the picture of innocence.

"Yes, I'll do that."

Was she *toying* with him? he wondered as he trotted down the stairs with all the upstairs curtains over his arm. The tingling sensation had reached his brain by this time, which was having a revisionist moment. Was it not clear, his brain told him, that her body language was unambiguously… unambiguous? On the other hand, he already knew that Spaniards were more tactile than most, so maybe they had just been friendly, brotherly or cousinly brushes. He debated this issue as he yanked down the remaining curtains and stuffed them all into a big cardboard box, but his only conclusion was that he quite fancied a bit more bodily contact before the cleaning was done. With this in mind, he strode back up the stairs to offer his services once more.

"Hmm, I'm going to start mopping the floors now, so you could go ahead, dusting things and moving the furniture, if you like," she said with that same serene smile.

"Yes, I'll do that," he said with a wider smile, seeing endless opportunities for further brushes. Maybe she would stumble at some point and he'd have to grasp her around the waist to prevent her from falling, or perhaps she would fall to the floor and he would have to gather her in his arms and comfort her.

In the event, and try as he might, he couldn't get within touching distance of her during the next two hours, mainly because a section of wet tiles usually came between them. No, the curtain removal had been a unique situation that wouldn't be repeated, unless he took the usual steps towards conscious and deliberate brushing, not to mention stroking and, a little further down the line, fondling, followed by kissing and even more intimate things that he couldn't quite imagine Ana doing, but then he hadn't expected her to brush against him twice either.

"There, that's a lot better, isn't it?" she said as they stood in the living room, breathing in the heady scent of chemical pine. She had sent him off to clean the bathroom while she did the kitchen, making him think that he might have been eyeing her a little too much. Was it a tactic to make his heart grow fonder? He wouldn't have thought her capable of that, but one never knew.

"That's great, Ana. I'd never have done all that myself, but I'll know what to do now when it gets dirty again," he said, rather foolishly, he knew, but he didn't want her to leave just yet. "How are you getting on with the booking system?"

"It's easy."

"You know, I mentioned to Eusebio that you ought to be the receptionist this summer."

"Ah."

"Yes, I mean, I think you'd be a lot more professional than him and, well, nicer to look at." He blushed and so did she, but not, he guessed, as much as him.

"Hmm, I think from next month it will get quite busy," she said. "I've been working there for almost three years and the hotel has never been full."

"Oh, where did you work before?" he asked, having assumed that she'd spent her entire adult life making beds.

"I worked in an office in Plasencia, but after the economic crash the company closed. The hotel was just something to tide me over, but I've been there for a while now," she said, the edges of her mouth turning down in a most appealing way, before another sunny smile unruffled her divine brow.

"I see. Well, in that case you should either work in reception or get another job, don't you think?"

"Yes. I didn't study administration in Badajoz for three years just to make beds, did I?"

"No, definitely not."

"I'll go now. Will you be moving in today?"

"Yes…" Nigel put his slightly numbed brain into gear. "I still have to do some more work on the hotel website, so I'll be seeing you."

"Right." She undid her apron and took it off in a rather languid manner which made her fine breasts rise and then fall.

Nigel looked up quickly. "I've no internet here yet, you see, so I'll ask Eusebio if I can use the hotel Wi-Fi to do my other stuff too."

"Don't you have a dongle?"

"A what? Oh, yes, but it's very slow."

"Ciao, Nigel," she said with a short, sweet smile, before turning on her heels and strolling out of the door.

When the image of her splendid bum finally left enough space in his brain to think of other things, he slumped into an armchair – he had three, but no sofa – and reviewed the morning's event. After a few moments' musing he concluded that all that had actually happened was that Ana had brushed her arm against his, twice, so it was really nothing to get excited about. She'd been to college too, which raised her score on his snobometer, but did either of those things make her more desirable than she had been before? He decided that they did, a bit, but that he would bide his time and try to engage her in conversation when he went to use Eusebio's Wi-Fi, though his dongle worked well enough.

After touring his new domain once more and finding that he had plenty of towels and bedlinen, he decided to go into Plasencia to buy a new duvet, duvet covers, sheets, pillows and pillowslips, as he would never know which sheets the former owner had slept between during his last night, nor for how much of that night he had spent growing cold. Silly, he knew, as life is but four days, figuratively speaking, but death wasn't something he wished to dwell on as he drifted off to sleep each night.

He had missed the midday bus, however, so he went to Fernando's for lunch, which he insisted on paying for, before joining Esteban at the bar for coffee.

"So you've come to a decent bar for a change," Nigel said as he slapped the hunched figure on his broad back.

"Ah, Neegel, it's you, or should I say Noi-gel?"

"Nai-gel."

"Nai-gel."

"Good, how are you doing?"

"Oh, killing time and looking forward to a life of poverty. It breaks my heart to see the expensive materials they are using on my bar. It isn't a palace, after all, but my father insists." He shook his head. "So, you are moving to old Juan's house, I believe?"

"Yes, today. Speaking of Juans, do you know the chap called Juan who sells cars?"

"Yes, and you too have met him."

"Have I?"

"Yes, he generally spends his evenings in Victor's bar."

"Oh."

"Yes, he liked to imitate your cry of 'yes, yes, yes' after the football match when you thought you were your own twin brother."

"Oh, God."

"But he stopped some time ago. You were very strange back then, though it's only a couple of weeks ago."

"Yes, I'd just come out of an asylum in Madrid."

"Really?"

"Yes, but for the moment you have no bar in which to spread the news, you old gossip. Of course I didn't, I was just a little…" He searched for the words for 'highly-strung'. "…a little stressed."

"I know, it has all been forgotten, Nai-gel," he said with a look that suggested that it was archived for future use should the occasion present itself. "So, do you wish to buy a car?"

"I think so, if I can find a cheap one that'll get me to Plasencia and back. I shan't be doing a lot of kilometres."

Nigel suspected that by buying a car his residence status might be called into question, but he decided to cross that bridge when he came to it.

Esteban looked at his watch. "He will be at Victor's having coffee."

"What does he look like?"

"I'll come with you. It will give me something to do."

Juan proved to be a small, dark, wiry man of about forty who worked for the village council, painting, litter picking, pruning trees, and generally keeping the place in order. His garage was a sideline of too little importance to bother the tax authorities with, and it just happened that he had acquired an excellent Renault Cinco from a careful lady owner only a few days ago.

"A Renault *Cinco*? But they're ancient."

"It is a Supercinco, of course, and is barely twenty years old. It has only done eighty thousand kilometres and still has plenty of paint," said Juan, his face becoming suddenly alert as he got into his sales patter.

"Plenty of paint?"

"Yes, it is a little faded by the sun, but fortunately it is white, and white cars suffer less."

"How much is it?"

"Oh, for you, as you are working for the good of the village, which I hope will make my job more interesting, you can have it for the same amount as I paid for it."

"How much?"

"Though I've changed the oil and filters."

"How much?"

"Seven hundred."

"Too much," Nigel said, draining his coffee glass. "I must go."

"Six-fifty then."

"I'll have a look around in Plasencia tomorrow."

"Six hundred, my final price."

"OK, if the car runs well."

"Like a dream. I finish work at seven. I can bring it round to the hotel at about eight."

"Nigel is now living in old Juan's house," said Esteban, still chuckling over the quick-fire haggling. He knew that Juan hadn't actually bought the car from the lady in question, but would still make a little money on the deal, and would be as good as his word regarding the oil and filters.

"Juan el Barbas?"

"Yes."

"A nice little house."

"Was that his name?" Nigel asked.

"His nickname," said Esteban.

"Oh, so he had a beard?" Nigel saw the corpse in a new light, a sort of cross between Tolstoy and Che Guevara.

"No, and nor did his father or grandfather. Our nicknames go back a long way and are passed from generation to generation," said Esteban.

"What's yours?"

"El Rojo."

"So you're a communist or something?"

"*I* vote for the Partido Popular," he said, referring to the conservative party. "But I believe my great-grandfather had different political views."

"What's yours, Juan?"

"El Mecánico."

"Ah, so you come from a family of mechanics."

"No, mine is new. My parents came here from a village in Salamanca."

"He's still an outsider," Esteban said, patting the interloper on the back.

"So what does that make me?"

"Oh, you are still young. When you marry and settle down with a local girl, you will begin to integrate into our little community," Esteban said with a wink.

"Why the wink?"

"Oh, nothing, but if you had spent the morning *alone* in a house with a single lady fifty years ago, you would have found yourself at the altar very quickly."

"Or if you had gone driving all day with one, only God knows where," added Juan with a grin.

"You guys are the pits," Nigel said in English with a placid smile.

"Qué?" they both asked.

"You're both very witty. What's Eusebio's nickname?"

"El Gitano."

"Really? He isn't a gypsy, is he?"

"No, but one suspects he must have some gypsy blood. He doesn't like it, by the way, as he is a terrible racist," said Juan.

"While my friend Bernardo, El Moro, doesn't mind his," said Esteban.

"So were his ancestors Moors?"

"Ha, all of us have some Moorish blood, I suppose."

"Not me," said Juan, though he was darker than most. "The Arabs spent little time in Salamanca before we pushed them down here to mix with the Christians and produce these strange Extremeño people."

All this idle chatter made Nigel almost forget that he still had to move his things, and Juan that he had to go back to work, so after agreeing to meet him with the Supercinco later at the house, Nigel took his leave and wandered back to the hotel.

It wasn't until about ten o'clock in the evening that he realised that he'd had a very busy day, but now with his possessions stored, his fridge and cupboards well-stocked, and an old, faded, but smooth-running car parked outside on the street, he went over the events of the day. It was nice to have his own place again, and the small house was far bigger than his outer London flat had been, but it was his new feelings regarding Ana that played most on his mind. He hadn't seen her at the hotel and would stay away the following day, but sooner or later he thought that things would come to a head. Maybe he would invite her to lunch at the weekend, away from the village of course, so they could get to know each other better, because he knew that at the hotel Eusebio's goggling eyes would never be far away.

He switched on the small, flat-screen TV and was disappointed that the football season had ended. Though football had never interested him, he had got used to seeing it in the bars and knew that it was usually the best option on Spanish television, as they could only fit in fifteen minutes of adverts at half time. Better to watch men running around after a ball than American films and series that always seemed to be dubbed by the same voices. He opened his laptop and slid in one of his Reginald Perrin DVDs. Leonard Rossiter's portrayal of a fugitive from corporate life was magnificent and Nigel's repeated viewing of the first two series may have played a part in provoking his past eccentricities. He wondered if Ana's mother looked like a hippopotamus, before reflecting that no real woman would possess the forbearance of Reginald's wife Elizabeth.

No, Reggie had played out a fine fantasy, but real life wasn't like that. Nigel wondered if he had done the right thing in renting the house, and decided that he had. He could leave whenever he liked and drive as far as his little car would take him, so he wasn't trapped at all. Realising that he hadn't made his bed, he went upstairs and selected two sheets, two pillowslips and a blanket from the cupboard. They all smelt fresh enough when he slipped between them a while later, and he would soon be able to dispense with the blanket for the summer. No thoughts of death assailed him as he lay gazing at the hideous purple lampshade that he would have to replace, and he was pleased not to have bought a duvet, because after the summer who knew what he might do? He could drive south, ditch the car, and head to Morocco for the winter, couldn't he? Of course he could, if he wanted to, but tomorrow he'd have to buy a plain lampshade and a bedside lamp.

9

The next morning, after arranging his surprisingly cheap car insurance, he drove into Plasencia, bought a few things, had breakfast on a café terrace in the square, and enjoyed the fact that he could drive back whenever he wished. The Plaza Mayor was every bit as splendid as that of Cáceres, and as the town also had its Roman Aqueduct, Moorish walls, and a colossal cathedral, the 'Places to Visit' leaflets that he was still planning would have to include a prominent page about the town.

"I'll get on with the leaflets now that I've settled in," he told Carla that afternoon in the shop.

"I was going to mention that house to you, so I'm glad Eusebio has sorted it out. As for the leaflets, I've got loads of photos for them, of here and all the places people ought to visit."

"Are they good one? I mean, they'll have to be top quality," he said, having little faith in his own or anyone else's photographic skills.

"Yes, my ex-husband took them, you see, and he's a photographer."

"Is he? You never mentioned him, so I didn't ask."

"He's living in Seville now, working for a newspaper there."

"Is he doing well?" Nigel asked out of politeness.

"I think so. The last time we spoke, a while ago, he said that the Sevillanos have so many processions and are so vain that he's never idle, though the work can be a little monotonous."

"So do you still get on all right?"

"Oh yes. We were just incompatible, but he's a good man. So, I can select the photos, and I suppose I'd better do the Spanish texts as I know the area better than you."

"Ha, just a little, not to mention the language. It was a bit presumptuous of me to suggest doing the leaflets, I suppose, but nobody else seemed to be interested."

"Most people here aren't interested in tourism one way or the other. It's only the hotel and bars who stand to gain anything, and maybe the shops."

"Well, one thing I am good at is putting the things together, so if you email me the photos and the texts, I'll design the leaflets and do an English version, shall I?"

"Yes, then we can get my Uncle Enrique to have them printed. The village will pay for that, of course."

"I suppose that's all we can do for the time being, isn't it? The village, hotel and restaurant websites are all very visible now and plenty of people are looking at them. Esteban will reopen in a couple of weeks and the hotel and all the bars will have new wooden signs, except Victor's, of course."

"Hmm, I know that Enrique has had a word with him, principally about hygiene and food quality, but I think he mentioned that horrible, cracked Coca-Cola sign too, so he may surprise us yet. What's wrong?" she asked, noticing his pensive frown.

"Oh, nothing. A week or so ago it seemed that I had loads of things to do, and now it looks like most of them will soon be done. What will I do with myself then?"

"You have your writing, don't you?"

"Yes, of course," he said, as like many novice writers he often forgot to write, especially if he had other distractions.

"Well, do some writing and enjoy yourself. The municipal pool opens this week. I'll put a photo of that in the village leaflet, of course."

"Will it not be full of noisy kids?"

"Well, they can be noisy at times, but there aren't so many kids here. You'll see that much of the time it's just as nice as a hotel pool. It's an asset to the village, thanks to Enrique."

"Yes, listen, we'll have to go out again sometime. We could go in my super new car."

"Ha, I know it. The lady drove it very little and now she's bought a new Fiat Panda. She's over sixty now and says it will be her last car."

"People don't seem to sell things as much here. In England people are always changed their cars and moving house. Do you have a housing ladder here?"

"What's that?"

"I guess you don't then," he said, before explaining the enslaving concept to her.

"How silly! My house is fine, so why would I move?"

Nigel had seen her house but wondered what it was like inside, because he still thought that something more than friendship might blossom between them. He enjoyed chatting to her and knew that Ana wasn't as conversationally gifted, but he sensed that if Carla rubbed her arm against his he wouldn't get quite the same tingly feeling, though of course he wouldn't know unless it happened.

'Carla, would you mind brushing past me just to see how it feels?' he thought of asking.

"You're dreaming, Nigel," she said with a chuckle.

"Oh, sorry. So, are you free this weekend?"

"Not this weekend, no. On Saturday I work, and on Sunday I'm going to visit a friend of mine in Talavera de la Reina."

"That's on the way to Madrid, isn't it? I passed through there on the bus here," he said, wondering who the friend was who warranted what must be a hundred and fifty mile round-trip.

"Yes, it's a girl I know… from university. I haven't seen her for a while."

"Right."

"Listen, why don't you ask Ana if she'd like to go for a drive with you?"

"Ana? From the hotel?"

"You know perfectly well which Ana I mean, Nigel," she said with a grin.

"Oh… oh, I don't think so," he said, still collecting his thoughts.

"Why not?"

"Well, she might… she might not…"

"What?"

"She might… read too much into it."

"Don't be silly. She's a grown woman and can look after herself. It will do her good to knock about with someone interesting for a change."

"Thanks."

"And, well, if you're not interested in her in… that way, you might be doing her a favour by taking her out."

"Oh, how's that?"

"Well, you're not a bad-looking chap, you know, and there are a few eligible men in the area who might prick up their ears if they hear she's been gallivanting about with the mysterious foreigner."

"Not so mysterious anymore, I hope."

"Hmm, you're still an enigma to many people. Anyway, I think Ana's got into a rut working at that damn hotel and I don't think her self-esteem has been great since she lost her proper job.

One way or another I think spending time with you will be good for her."

"Er, Carla, how well do you know Ana?"

"Oh, not well. She was a few classes below me at school, you see, but we have a chat when we see each other. Off you go now. Sra Martínez has walked past three times already."

"Email me the photos and the text."

"I will do."

On Wednesday, Thursday and Friday evenings Carla emailed him photos and sections of text, so he composed the leaflets little by little and also did the English translation. He could ask his sister to help him with a French version if he felt there was a demand for it, though other languages would have to wait until the village's tourist destination status was confirmed, if that ever happened.

On Saturday morning he went along to the local pool and was so impressed by what he saw that he bought a seasonal pass there and then. The place had looked bare before it had opened, but now with the pool, picnic tables and benches uncovered, sunbeds scattered about, the tiny bar open, a dozen people frolicking in the water, supervised by an earnest young lifeguard in his highchair, and as many more lazing about on the grass, it was a pleasant, relaxing place to be. Why pay for an expensive hotel, he thought, when you could stay at a relatively cheap place like Eusebio's and stroll a few hundred yards to a perfectly good pool? There were views of the plains to the south and the mountains to the north, and the fresh air and negligible traffic noise made it seem like a veritable oasis that would hopefully help him to while away the summer.

The water was still cold, he found on diving in, but he had been assured that the stifling summer heat was just around the corner, so he felt pretty good as he lay on his towel on the grass, letting the sun's rays warm his unevenly tanned body. This is the life, he was thinking when a cloud obscured the sun, only it wasn't a cloud, but a stout young man dressed incongruously in a shirt, tie, sharply creased trousers and shiny black shoes.

"Excuse me, are you the Englishman?" he asked in English.

"I am English, yes," he replied in Spanish, before sitting up and shading his eyes.

The balding man in his early thirties crouched down and held out his hand. "Soy Javier."

"Nigel." He took the curiously clammy hand, which had probably been on the steering wheel of an air conditioned car very recently. "How can I help you?" he asked, as the man carried no towel.

"Well, I represent some business interests in this part of the country and I heard that you too were considering investing in rural tourism here."

"Who told you that?"

"Fernando at the restaurant. I often lunch there when I am in the area."

Nigel suppressed an urge to utter an oath, mainly in order to see what the crafty-looking chap was up to. "Oh, yes, Fernando, a good friend of mine."

"Yes, a fine man, and a good judge of character," he said with a sickly smile. He was generally overweight, but his face and neck were fatter than the rest of him, and his lips were especially blubbery. Nigel didn't like him and decided to revert to his filmmaking days for a while.

"Well, Javier… oh, please take a seat," he said, pointing at the grass.

"Can we talk elsewhere… Nigel?"

"Walls have ears, Javier," he said through slit-like eyes, before laying down a fleece top for him to sit on.

He sat down and loosened his tie, as the sun was burning down.

Nigel crossed his legs, interlaced his fingers, and cleared his throat. "Well, Javier, I came here initially looking for a place to make a documentary film. I... collaborate with a German production company and the project has been set in motion, but I always have an eye open for investment opportunities and when I arrived here I thought it might be a good place to promote rural tourism, as Fernando so rightly told you."

"I see, and do you still think it a suitable location?"

"Hmm, I don't know." He tipped his head from side to side and pursed his lips, before looking at him sharply. "What do *you* think, Javier?"

"We... well, I think it *looks* like a good place, but then so do so many other villages."

"That's true," Nigel said, his eyes wandering over to the pool. "Tell me, what do your investors have in mind?"

"Well, that depends."

"On what?" he asked, still looking away.

"Well, at the moment we lack inside information."

"Such as?"

"Well, who might sell land, how easy it would be to gain building permission, and... things like that."

Nigel looked at him and saw globules of sweat beginning to form on his head, which was getting redder by the minute.

"Yes, those are crucial factors, of course."

"Can we not go into the bar for a drink?"

Nigel tapped his nose and passed him the sun cream, which he declined.

"I envisage, initially, a chalet complex over there, beyond the first oak trees," Nigel said, pointing to an especially picturesque spot.

"Ah, yes, a good place. How many chalets?"

"Oh, twenty or so, at first, with a pool about the size of this one, and a decent restaurant."

"I see," he said, his fat lips forming a smile.

"I calculate that my partners and I could fund half of the development, if we could find Spanish investors for the other half. In Bulgaria we found it… expedient to collaborate with local investors, as they invariably know how to deal with all the little inconveniences which inevitably arise."

"Yes, yes, that's what we find," he said with enthusiasm, before knocking a drop of sweat from his nose. "National expertise is always best, in legal matters."

"Precisely. That is all agricultural land, of course, and impossible to build on, technically."

"Technically, yes," he said, nodding a few more drops off.

"Luckily I have got to know the village mayor very well during my short time here."

"Ah, I asked Fernando about him, but he told me to come and find you first."

"Did he?" Nigel asked, striving to keep the surprise he felt out of his voice. Maybe Fernando wasn't such a numpty after all and had purposely sent the flabby minion of unknown predators to see the person he thought most likely to lead him on a wild goose chase. It was him who had started the whole rural tourism rumour in the first place, so Fernando was right to send the man along to the horse's mouth. Enrique had stated that if any new tourist accommodation were to be established, it ought to be on a small scale and with local money, so Nigel knew exactly where the mayor stood on the issue. He also knew that he had a good sense of humour.

"It was quite right of him to send you to see me. Enrique, the mayor, and I are like that." He moved the index and middle fingers of his right hand together a few time. "But he doesn't like to be bothered with people who waste his time, Javier."

"Oh, I *assure* you I wouldn't be wasting his time," he said, alert and a little drier after passing a handkerchief over his head. "We have the means to back a project of the size you mention, but it depends largely on the... malleability of the local officials." He raised his eyebrows and grinned, horribly.

As Nigel was enjoying himself, he decided to save his punchline for a little longer. "The project I mentioned is just the start, of course."

"Oh?"

"Yes, to get a foothold, you know. It is essential to have a foothold before you propose the golf course."

"A *golf* course?"

"Of course. Did I not mention that?"

"No."

"I'm sorry, it slipped my mind. It must be the heat. Yes, my German, Swedish and Belgian friends and I aren't interested in a few chalets. What's the point in that? No, we get our foothold, then our golf course, and later, when the land has been reclassified, we surround the golf course with dozens and dozens of chalets, ha ha," he cackled. "The stupid locals say, 'Hey, what's happened here?' but by then it's too late. Oh, we've done that in Almería, Málaga and Murcia, before the crash, of course, but it wasn't our problem by then. Now the time is ripe to begin again. Are you *with* me, Javier?" he asked, staring at him and clamping his teeth together, lest he burst out laughing.

"Yes... I think so. I will have to consult my associates, of course."

"The *first* thing you have to do is to go and see the mayor."

"Yes, after I've–"

"Without delay." He pulled his mobile phone from his shorts pocket and speed-dialled Enrique. "Enrique! How's it going, old pal? Listen, where are you now? ... At the village hall? Brilliant. I'm going to send a *very* interesting chap round to see you right away ... Yes, he's the man we've been waiting for ... Dead serious, yes, so you treat him right, eh? Reassure him that there won't be any petty red tape and a year from now you and me will be in the Seychelles, just like we planned. What? ... Yes, yes, he'll be round right away. Call me later. Ciao, Enrique!" He dropped the phone and beamed at Javier.

"I really need to speak–"

"Off you go. There isn't a moment to lose. In an hour's time he'll be drunk in the bar. Have you got a sweetener?"

"A what?"

"A sweetener, you know, a little envelope, but not too little, eh?"

"Well, no..."

"Don't worry. Bring a few thousand next time."

"Are you not coming?"

"Me? No, no, me and Enrique never meet in daylight. *Far* too risky. Not everyone in the village wants a golf course, you know, especially not the farmers, ha, ha!"

"I'll go round then," he said weakly, before pushing himself up in an equally feeble manner.

Nigel jumped up, patted him on the back, and squeezed his hand with about half his strength, which was enough to make him wince. Another more vigorous pat on the back sent him stumbling towards the entrance.

Enrique, who hadn't got a word in edgeways on the phone, sat waiting for the man in gleeful anticipation, for he had never taken a bribe in his life.

A blue BMW was soon seen rolling through the village, driven by a man pouring with sweat, before he hit the gas on the outskirts and sped away towards the motorway.

"Did you deal with that fat rogue?" Fernando asked Nigel as he laid the table.

"Oh yes, it was just like old times. Enrique will be along shortly."

The hairy mayor soon appeared, dressed in a checked shirt and jeans. "Our investor never arrived," he said with a grin.

"No, I didn't think he would. I think his bosses sent him out, sniffing around for opportunities," Nigel said, before reproducing their conversation as accurately as he could.

"Ha, I'm glad you enjoyed yourself, and sorry that I was unable to give him a piece of my mind. I saw a lot of people like that ten or fifteen years ago, and a couple of them really did have envelopes of money ready for me, but they soon saw that I wasn't that kind of mayor."

"It makes you think though, doesn't it? A rumour gets around and people are prepared to act on it."

"Yes, some of these capitalists are just as gullible as the folk they intend to cheat."

Fernando came back to take their order, and only when he had brought the wine, salad and basket of bread did Enrique continue.

"There is potential here, however, to offer more accommodation to tourists, but it must be done with the good of the village in mind. I'd like to see less young people having to drive to work in Plasencia, and going to live there and further afield, so the objective must be to create local jobs."

"Through local investment?"

"Exactly. Eusebio tells me that he already has more bookings than ever before. Normally he's only busy in August, mainly with Spanish holidaymakers, but this year he'll be busy from now until… well, at least October."

"Foreign tourists will come during at least six months of the year. After a winter in Britain even April seems wonderful here, despite the cold nights." Nigel sipped his wine and waited for Enrique to speak.

"And how do you think we should proceed, Nigel?"

"Well, if you look up more touristic villages online, they have more hotels and guesthouses, of course, but also private rural houses for rent."

"Hmm, there are a few farmhouses lying idle within a few kilometres of here."

"Completely empty?"

"A couple aren't used at all, and others… well, the owners spend some time there in summer, but mainly to stop them falling down. With the big tractors, quad bikes and other machinery, small farms are no longer viable. Some farmers have bought more land, but they have no use for the houses. One fine house I know is now used solely to house the pigs in winter."

"What? Like factory farming?"

"Oh no, not our pigs, they merely sleep indoors when the nights are freezing. A cheap metal barn would be sufficient, but as the owner has no other use for the house, he allows them to ruin it. That's his business, of course, but I'm sure at least a couple of the house owners could be persuaded to invest in rural tourism if they were sure it would be profitable."

"Yes, a house could be rented outright, or divided into apartments, maybe with a small pool too. That's how things are done elsewhere."

"We must begin to spread this idea around the village, you and I. People like to believe they have thought things out for themselves, so to approach the owners directly would be a mistake. Our propaganda must, of course, be both subtle and serious," he said, his white teeth smiling through his beard.

"Oh yes, I shan't be saying any more stupid things, unless another opportunity like today's presents itself. Then there's the village itself. A village called Jerte that Carla took me to see is smaller than this one, but has several places for people to stay."

"Hmm, Jerte is up nearer to the mountains, and that area is now an established destination," Enrique said with a frown. "Rome wasn't built in a day, and nor was Jerte."

"No, but I'm sure one more hotel or guesthouse would be successful here. Can you think of anywhere suitable, or anyone who would be prepared to invest the money? Ideally it would open before next Easter."

"Hmm, one place springs to mind. Do you know the big old house on the main road, about a hundred metres from Sara's bar?"

"The white one? Well, the one that used to be white?" Nigel asked, thinking of a large detached house with about eight front windows, some of them boarded up, set back from the road.

"Yes, that was the notary's house, back in the days when we had a notary. It's almost as big as Eusebio's hotel, but would require a large investment."

"Who owns it?"

"As far as I know, the descendants of the last notary."

"When did he leave?"

"In the early thirties, I think, when the republic was established."

"Right, so the whole place will need refurbishing."

"Yes. I'll make some enquiries regarding the owners. I believe they still pay the rates each year, so Marta should be able to find their telephone number," he said, referring to the dumpy, middle-aged lady who performed administrative duties at the village hall three mornings a week. "I'll ask them if they wish to sell."

"And then what?"

"That depends on what they say. Some people like to hold onto property forever, or until an opportunity arises, so I mustn't let them know our plans."

"You could say that the village council wishes to buy it, for storage space or something."

"Yes, but that would be lying."

"Yes, sorry, I suppose it would."

Enrique wound a wisp of his beard around his finger and remained silent when Fernando arrived with the plates of lamb chops and chips. From then on Eduardo attended to them, as it had become clear to the owner that there was no gossip to be gleaned.

"What you say makes me think, however, that I might not be the best person to call them," he finally said.

"Oh?"

"No, if I call they may suspect that the village does have plans for the building and they will ask a higher price. If, on the other hand, you were to call, as a private individual who is looking for, I don't know…"

"An old building to store my hang-gliders in?"

"What?"

"Ha, it's just an example. I mean, I could stress that I don't intend to restore the building, but merely to use it for some type of storage. I think I'd be able to show enough indifference to assure them that they don't possess a goldmine."

"Yes, you are good at that sort of thing," he laughed.

"How much do you think they'll ask?"

"Well, as it is, and with house prices still very low around here, I don't think it's worth more than fifty or sixty thousand."

"Hmm, that's still quite a lot. It might be cheaper to buy some land and build from scratch."

"Yes, there are plots available, but not in such prominent places," said Enrique.

"And I suppose it would look quite elegant with the walls and roof restored. Foreign tourist like old buildings. Is there land with it?"

"There's a large courtyard at the back, with a few oak trees, I believe."

"Hmm, a nice patio for the guests."

They concentrated on their meal for a while and dropped the subject until coffee was served. Nigel was thinking hard about the rather stately old building and Enrique didn't interrupt him.

"Shall I give you the telephone number then?" he asked as he poured a little brandy into his coffee.

"Yes, the first thing is to call them. They might ask a fortune, or not want to sell at all."

"And if the price is reasonable?"

"Then we could meet here next Saturday and talk about it some more," Nigel said, unwilling to share the rather daring idea that he had been mulling over. Instead he told him that the two leaflets would soon be ready and that he ought to order a thousand of each.

"A thousand?"

"Yes, that will be enough to start with. We can always print some more later on."

"Right. Email me the templates and I'll see to it one evening this week."

10

After a Sunday spent walking, swimming, sunbathing, reading and writing, Nigel sprang into action on Monday morning. He drove his surprisingly nippy car into Plasencia at eight o'clock and spent two hours at the police station, sorting out his residence papers. He had studied the procedure online and by proving that he had sufficient funds to support himself for a long time, his provisional resident status was granted. From there he went to a bank, opened an account, and deposited the cheque for €40,000 that his mother had given him from her life insurance windfall. After putting fifty euros' credit on his phone, he called his two banks in England to check his accounts. The balance on the account he had been using stood at just over £22,000, the remains of his hard-earned savings from his London years, while his deposit account contained a healthy £131,432.

No-one knew about this account, not even his generous mother, but then no-one knew about the 50p accumulator bet that he had won on an online betting site that he had joined in a moment of ennui the previous autumn. He had placed a few quick-fire bets before closing the page in disgust at his pointless action, but a week later he learnt that the random results he had chosen for that weekend's Norwegian Premier League fixtures had proven to be correct. On studying his predictions more closely, he realised that it really was a minor miracle that Sogndal had beaten Brann away from home, and that Tromsø had done likewise at Rosenborg, but he thought it a kindly twist of fate that just after handing in his notice at work – on the strength of his mother's gift – this miracle had occurred. In the short term it did nothing to improve his mental health, as we have seen, but now that the time for action was nigh he was very grateful for his undeserved nest egg.

He had decided to buy the old house on the main road, assuming it was for sale and the price wasn't excessive. As he still didn't have the owners' telephone number he might have spent his time studying other options, but he didn't because he felt that the house was just right. He had walked past it the day before and looked into a few of the rooms. The high ceilings and decorative plasterwork had appealed to him, as had the rear patio, which did indeed contain four holm-oak trees, which someone must have been pruning, and harvesting the acorns, because they were still manageable after almost ninety years.

He had thought then that a couple of piglets trotting around would amuse the future guests, but as he sat under the shade of a parasol at a café in the Plaza Mayor he had no such flights of fancy. He would buy the house, if he could, but what he would do with it he didn't know. Were he to set about restoring it to anywhere near its former glory he would tie himself down for at least a year and spend a large proportion of his remaining savings, if not all of them, as he hadn't a clue how much building work cost to carry out. No, he would buy it and decide what to do with it later. The rush he felt as he sat in the square was out of proportion to the alcohol content of the beer he was sipping, and the mere thought of performing such a daring action made him feel more alive than ever.

Until then he had been an earner, not a spender, as he didn't count the thousands of pounds he had frittered away on rent and commuting over the last few years as spending. No, that was pure drudgery, even a kind of slavery, but this would be different. It wasn't about the pride he would feel on owning such an off-white elephant, though the idea did tickle him, but about the dynamic nature of his proposed action. Pretending to be a filmmaker or his own twin brother was pure nonsense compared to taking the first steps towards dragging his adopted home into the twenty-first century. In years to come, when the village was a modest but thriving centre of tourism, people would say, 'Do you remember Nigel, the man who made all this happen?' 'Yes, *he* saw our potential, and now our school is full once more, as the young people can stay.' 'A fine man.' 'Yes, a splendid chap.'

And where would Nigel Hamson be then? he asked himself as he tossed a couple of coins into the tray and stood up. Well, that remained to be seen, but buying a house needn't tie him down any more than it had the notary and his descendants.

He returned to the bank and arranged to transfer another €40,000 into his new Spanish account, before going shopping for lampshades, a rug for his bedroom floor, and a bedside light.

It wasn't until Wednesday evening that Enrique called Nigel to give him the telephone number of the owner of the house.

"She's called Sra Muñoz Puig, so it sounds like her mother's side of the family is Catalan, which is bad news, Nigel."

"Why's that?"

"Because they're very shrewd, the Catalans, not to say tight-fisted, but she lives in Madrid, so we might be lucky."

"I hope so."

"Oh, and I've ordered the leaflets, which should arrive within a week. Two thousand sounds rather a lot."

"Don't worry, Enrique, they won't be sitting in Eusebio's hotel gathering dust. I'll let you know what the lady says."

"You do that, and good luck."

On hanging up, Nigel sensed that Enrique suspected that he intended to buy the old house, and that he approved of the idea. As it was only eight o'clock he decided to call her right away. A child answered the phone, before handing it over to a woman who sounded no older than himself.

"Sra Muñoz? Hola, I'm calling about the old house which you own in the village."

"Which village?" she asked in a clear, pleasant voice.

Nigel was more specific.

"Oh, that old thing. I think I saw a photo of it once. Is it still standing?"

"Yes, just about," Nigel said equally pleasantly. "I wondered if you'd thought about selling it."

"To tell the truth, I hadn't thought about it at all," she said with a refined titter. "I believe my husband's great-grandfather bought properties all over the place. What do you want it for?"

"Well…" Nigel had planned to say that he wished to pull the old, decrepit, ugly and downright dangerous eyesore down and build a humble dwelling for himself, his Spanish wife, and their four small children. He'd even considered mentioning that the house would be a bungalow, as he used a wheelchair, but that would be a last resort which he doubted he would have the nerve to resort to. Instinct, however, made him change his mind, so he said something else instead.

"I wish to restore the house. I want to promote rural tourism in the village and create jobs for local people."

"Oh, that sounds jolly nice," she said, or words to that effect, as she was clearly quite a posh young lady. "And how much do you think the old place is worth?"

"Well, it's in a bad state, and a builder has told me that it will cost over a hundred thousand to restore it, so I can only offer you forty thousand for the house, I'm afraid," he said, crossing his fingers and grimacing.

"Hmm, it's a handy sum of money, I suppose. So you plan to turn it into a hotel, do you?"

"Yes, or tourist apartments, but probably an economical hotel. It's a nice area to visit, don't you think?"

"I don't know. Where is it?"

"Er, near Plasencia."

"Ah, in Extremadura."

"Yes. I guess it was your husband's great-grandfather who was the notary here."

"I expect so. He did lots of things, by all accounts. Anyway, I must consult my husband, so I'll call you back on this number, shall I?"

"Yes, please do. I'm ever so keen to get started on the project, you see, as I want to get it finished before next summer," he found himself saying.

"How nice. Maybe we'd have a run over there one day if it happened. I expect we'd spend the night there, so you'd have to give us a discount, ha ha," she said in her singsong voice.

"Oh, I certainly would. If you sell you'll be doing us a big favour. Unemployment is still quite high here, you see."

"It is here in Madrid too. My husband was in building and laid off many workers after the crash."

"I'm sorry."

"Oh, *he's* all right. He's into renewable energy now, among other things. It's always the poor who suffer, isn't it?"

"Yes, usually."

"Very well, I shall call you later on."

Expecting either a very short or very long conversation with her husband, he plugged in his phone and went to admire the new canvas lampshades which had improved the look of the rooms remarkably. Shouldn't he be thinking about buying a practical place like this, rather than the money pit that he'd set his heart on? That probably wouldn't happen, in any case, not if her husband was a wealthy businessman. She sounded lovely and might have let it go for forty, but businessmen gave nothing away. Fifty was his limit, Nigel decided, as he really had been told that it would cost a heck of a lot to do the place up, especially if he wanted to create the en suite rooms that folk expected these days.

By ten o'clock he began to fear that the capitalist pig of a husband wouldn't even deign to call him back. He would sit on the property until prices were high again and then let it go. He might even set up a hotel there himself, as these parasitical entrepreneurs always stole other people's ideas. In the unlikely event of this happening, it shouldn't really bother him, as what did it matter who owned the hotel, as long as it created jobs and brought in the tourists? It did bother him though, and when the phone finally rang at a quarter past ten he was close to despising the man whose deep voice he heard on the line.

"So, you want to buy my great-grandfather's old townhouse, do you?"

There he was, the swine, already asserting the ties that he didn't feel, Nigel thought, before forcing himself to smile.

"Yes, I'm interested in it," he said, as there was no point appealing to this vulture's finer instincts.

"Hmm, and my wife tells me that you wish to make it into a hotel."

"Yes, that's the idea… to create jobs here, you know."

"Hmm, it won't create many jobs, will it?"

"Won't it? I mean, yes, it'll create quite a few. Receptionists, cleaners… er waiters, and a few others," he said, before scowling at the phone through which such sweet tones had emanated only two hours earlier.

"Waiters?" he asked with a grave chuckle. He sounded much older than his wife, so he'd probably dazzled her with his wealth, before snatching her straight from finishing school, the damned cad.

"Yes, waiters, and waitresses, for the restaurant."

"And where do you propose to situate this restaurant, my friend?"

"On the ground floor, of course. It's a big house, you know."

"I know, I have the plans before me, and I assure you there is no room for a restaurant."

What's it to you, pal? Nigel thought. "Is it for sale, or not?" he asked, wishing to repeat his offer and have done with it.

"Why not turn the place into a hostel?" he then asked, which made Nigel look at the phone and screw up his face.

"Well, a hotel, a hostel, what's the difference?"

"I mean a kind of youth hostel, perhaps somewhere that youngsters from the city could use, to get a taste of rural life."

"Hmm, that's one option."

"It would be much easier, and more beneficial, I think. Let me see." Nigel heard a rustling noise. "Yes, you could have the kitchen, dining room and communal space on the ground floor, and dormitories and bathrooms upstairs. The existing bathrooms are very large, so you could easily install… maybe three showers and three toilets in each, one for the boys and one for the girls, while the smaller bathroom downstairs would be for the staff. I doubt it would cost more than fifty thousand to restore the place in that way, assuming that the roof is sound."

"It doesn't look too bad," Nigel said weakly. Maybe he had misjudged the guy, or was there a killer blow about to descend? "Yes, I'll certainly think about that idea, but how much do you want for the property?"

"That depends."

Here we go, he thought. "On what?" he asked as pleasantly as he could.

"On what you intend to do with it. If you agree to go ahead with the idea I've suggested, the house is yours for €30,000."

"Right."

"That is extremely cheap, you know."

"Yes, but what if I decided to make it into a normal hotel?"

"Then you would pay the market price. I would send a man round to value it and let you know in due course, but I imagine, off the top of my head, that it would ascend to seventy or eighty thousand, considering the size of the place and its prominent situation."

"I don't know what to say," Nigel said, quite truthfully.

"I think you like my initial idea," said the still nameless man.

"Yes, I like it, but I don't know much about youth hostels."

"You are concerned that no-one would come, but you needn't worry about that. I will put my wife on the phone now."

"What? Oh, all right."

"Hola, Sr Hamson?"

"Nigel."

"Nigel, my husband and I have been discussing your proposal for some time. I'm sorry we kept you waiting."

"Oh, that's all right."

"I work for the Department of Education here in the Community of Madrid, you see, and one of our initiatives is to send underprivileged children for holidays in the country."

"Oh, I see."

"Most of our current destinations are east of Madrid, mainly in Valencia and Murcia, but it would be nice for them to see the Extremaduran grasslands too. You know, all those pigs and other animals."

"Sra Muñoz…"

"Lourdes."

"Lourdes, this is a lot of information to take in."

"Ha, yes. Well, I'll simplify matters, shall I? If you promise to convert the house into a hostel, I can guarantee that several groups will come from here every summer. Other regions have similar schemes, so I'm sure the project would be a success for the village."

The word village gave Nigel's whirring brain a jolt and he suddenly saw how he ought to proceed.

"This is really interesting, Lourdes, but I think I'll ask the mayor to call you tomorrow. He's as keen as I am to stimulate new initiatives in the village, and in view of what you've said, I think he's the man to take things forward."

"Hmm, I don't know how long you've been in Spain, Nigel, but there are mayors and mayors."

"Ours is one of the good ones, incorruptible and…" He pictured Enrique's smiling face surrounded by all that hair. "…well, he's been mayor for almost twenty years and the people still love him."

"In that case, yes, I'd like to speak to him. I'll give you my office number, shall I?"

"Yes, but he works away during the day. He doesn't get paid for being mayor, you see. Could he call you tomorrow evening?"

"Of course. Any time after seven. How fortuitous that you called us, don't you think?"

"Yes, I do. Thanks, Lourdes."

"Thank *you*, Nigel."

It was too late to call Enrique, as he set off for work at six in the morning, so he sent him a text message instead, which read, *Exciting news about the house. Please call me. Nigel.*

Enrique called him at ten the next morning. Nigel explained the situation and the mayor agreed to call Lourdes that evening.

"Let me know how it goes, Enrique."

"These matters require much reflection, Nigel. Let's meet at Fernando's on Saturday at two."

"Very well, see you then," he said, feeling a little disappointed by his friend's apparent lack of enthusiasm, though he later reflected that such proposals would be nothing new to a mayor of twenty years' standing.

On Friday Nigel finally decided to put in an appearance at the hotel, partly because his dongle had run out of credit, but mostly in the hope of seeing Ana. He had decided to ask her out for lunch and get to know her better. Assuming she agreed, he would whisk her away from the village in his car, sure that it would create no more gossip than chatting to her at the hotel, as there Eusebio would undoubtedly be as ubiquitous as ever, he thought as he walked through the door.

"Ah, Nigel, how nice to see you," he said, looking genuinely busy behind his reception desk.

"The wooden signs look great. How are things going?"

"Like never before. I have seven rooms occupied right now and my bookings for the summer continue to increase. I shall need more cleaning staff, I think."

"Good, so that means that Ana will be able to work on reception, won't she?"

"Well, yes, she does already."

"Where is she now?"

"Cleaning rooms."

"Until when?"

"Oh, until lunchtime, I imagine."

"No, I mean when does she stop cleaning rooms and take up her full reception duties?" Nigel asked sternly.

"Soon," Eusebio said weakly.

"Eusebio, despite your success being entirely down to *me*, I see that the sole beneficiary of your increased trade is going to be *you*," he said, slipping easily into acting mode.

"No, I–"

"Eusebio, Ana is not a cleaner. She has relevant studies and the right aptitudes to run the hotel far better than you. If I don't see her behind reception the next time I come here I will press two buttons on my computer and your website and bookings system will disappear from the face of the earth." He lifted an omnipotent finger and prodded the desk hard, twice.

Eusebio looked at the finger. "You won't do that, Nigel."

"Of course I won't, because from next week you will be employing Ana purely as a receptionist, won't you?" He stared into Eusebio's cowed eyes and gritted his teeth. It was far easier and more effective to pretend to be angry than to genuinely lose one's rag, he thought as his eyes drilled into the man's emaciated skull.

"Yes, Nigel."

"Good."

"But there is little space behind here. Where am I to go?"

Nigel looked around the reception area and his calmer eyes lit upon the old faux-leather sofa and two armchairs. "Over there, but not on them."

"What?"

"Get rid of those monstrosities and buy some wicker furniture, with cushions." He strode across the shiny floor with his hands behind his back like a young army officer. "A sofa here, another here, and four chairs. You'll have more guests hanging around, so you need more seating. Put a small TV up there on that pillar, then you can sit here in comfort and spring into action when guests arrive, and leave most of the work to Ana. How does that sound?"

"Expensive."

"Bah! You old miser," he said with a grin. "Do as I say and you won't regret it. Have I been wrong yet?"

"No, Nigel, you haven't," he said, picturing his new reception area.

"Whereabouts is Ana?"

"On the first floor, I think."

"I'm just going to nip up and have a word," he said, before striding up the stairs before Eusebio's expression changed from one of contrition to his usual lewd goggling. He must be a terrible miser, Nigel thought, because he would clearly enjoy Ana's presence in reception.

Ana was in the first of his old rooms, mopping the floor, so he tapped on the door and stood in the doorway.

"Hola, Nigel," she said with a smile.

"Hola, I see you're enjoying your reception duties."

"Ha, I spend about two hours a day behind there, doing all the work that he cannot do."

"Not for much longer," he said, before relating his recent theatricals.

"Oh, Nigel, you're so wicked!"

"He needed telling. Ana, do you feel like coming for a drive on Sunday? We could go somewhere for lunch."

She pursed her lips and looked thoughtful. "Well, yes, I don't see why not. What time?"

"At eleven? Where shall I pick you up?"

"I'll walk round to yours." She gave him an inscrutable look, before smiling and leaning on her mop. "I'd better get on. I've three more rooms to do."

"All right. Until Sunday at eleven then."

"Yes, see you then."

After checking his emails and reminding Eusebio to find a new cleaner without delay, he strolled home in a ruminative mood. He had expected Ana to be a bit more thrilled about their maiden outing, but in some ways he was glad that she hadn't jumped for joy. He still wasn't sure if it was the right thing to do, but his car was small and he was sure that when he felt her close his instinct would tell him how to act. From his house they could drive straight out of the village, which was probably why she had suggested meeting there, so all in all it was the best possible plan. He only hoped that he would have exciting news to tell her about the youth hostel project, in which he intended her to be involved, touch wood.

11

As he was going to have lunch at Fernando's, Nigel went to Sara's for coffee after his bracing morning swim. Her new wooden sign was up too, and her new bathrooms – one of which was finished – would be a great improvement, so he thought she had done enough for the time being. He told her he would bring some leaflets soon and headed back into the village. Despite being a Saturday, there was a lot of activity in and around Esteban's bar, so he popped his head through the door. Curiously enough, though the building work was still in progress, Esteban stood in his usual place behind the refurbished bar, while his father sat upon three boxes of tiles in the same spot where his domino table had stood.

"Those tiles on that wall don't look straight, young man," the old man said to one of the three workers.

"Grandfather, it is your eyes that don't see straight," the lad of twenty said with a grin. "Come and check with the spirit level, if you want."

"Bah! I don't trust those things. A plumb line was always good enough for me."

"Papá, let the boy get on with his work," said Esteban. "So, Nigel, you have come to witness my ruin."

"It's looking good already. When will you reopen?"

"In two weeks, God willing."

I didn't know you were pious, Esteban."

"I'm not, but I'm praying that all my customers come back," he said with a rueful look.

"They will. I for one am looking forward to lunching in my favourite bar again. This is the first one that the tourists at the hotel will see when they go for a stroll, so I'm sure some will come, especially for dinner."

"For dinner? I don't do dinners, unless there are a few tapas left."

"Well, in that case, serve them a drink and then point them in the direction of Fernando's. *He* will give them dinner," Nigel said, keen to get any flippancy out of his system before meeting Enrique and hearing his news.

"I can't do everything. I'd need to employ a cook."

"Not necessarily. There are several youngsters home from university now. You could employ one to work behind the bar, while you cook up your culinary marvels in the kitchen," he said, before deciding to err on the side of caution, as there were only twelve rooms in the hotel after all. "At least be prepared to offer dinner, in case the guests come over."

"I will bear it in mind. I have much to think about just now," Esteban said, leaning on his new bar in exactly the same place as he did before.

"Don't worry, you'll soon have your beer pump beside you and your customers before you."

After promising to bring leaflets and to put photos of the finished bar on the village website, he said goodbye and went home to change.

When he saw Enrique sitting up at the bar in Fernando's he tried to guess if the news about the house was positive, but the mayor was a discrete man and they talked only about commonplace things while they drank their small bottles of beer and ate a few olives. Only when they were seated and Eduardo had brought over the wine, bread and salad, did he broach the subject of the house.

"I have spoken to the owners three times now," he said.

"Really?"

"Yes, twice on the phone and once on Skype."

"She's nice, isn't she?"

"They are both good people. I suggested a video call as I wanted to see them. It isn't the same as being together in a room, but it's better than nothing. I had no doubts about her sincerity, but I wished to see how he looked and acted."

"He sounded like a typical businessman to me, at first anyway."

"That is undoubtedly what he is, but he wishes to please his wife, so…" He held out his hands, palms up.

"So what's the plan?"

"There are two possible courses of action, Nigel. The first is that you buy the house, refurbish the house, and run the business, which I'm sure will be profitable, as the lady, Lourdes, has many useful contacts."

Nigel gulped. "What's the second course of action?"

"That the village council buys the house, refurbishes it, and runs the business."

"Right."

"With you as manager, of course."

"But I don't know anything about running a hostel, Enrique."

"You don't know anything about filmmaking either, but after two days here you and your friend looked like professionals, in most people's eyes."

"Oh, yes, well, that was just to stir things up and get people thinking. I was sure that tourists would come, you see, but Esteban and company didn't believe me," he said, feeling extremely glad that the hotel was filling up.

"Ha, when I saw that video camera I knew your friend Stefan wasn't a professional. I have one very much like it, you see." He sipped his wine and licked his lips. "Anyway, sometimes it's a case of who dares wins, isn't it?"

"I guess so. I'm still not sure about managing the hostel though."

Enrique leant his head to one side and gazed at Nigel. "Because you don't want to feel trapped?"

"Well... yes."

"It will probably be closed from November to March, as it's far too cold here in winter. In any case, you can choose your degree of involvement. I think you're the person who needs to decide that. You could manage the whole concern, or choose an area of work that suits you, but unless you're a millionaire I think you need to think about earning some money."

"I know. I feel well-off right now, but I haven't got that much, about €200,000, in fact," he said, feeling that he owed him a sign of his sincerity.

"Hmm, a nice sum of money, but then you don't possess a house and you're still young. So, the first course of action, which I suggested because it was your idea, is not viable. These things always cost more than one expects and I can only manage it because I have a good reputation in the Junta de Extremadura and can secure the funds."

"I think I'd like to work with the kids, or youngsters, who come to stay. Lourdes said they'd be underprivileged though, so I'm not sure what the villagers will think if they go running around the place."

"Ha, I think Lourdes's idea of underprivileged and ours are two different things. For holidays of this type there are grants available for families whose incomes aren't high. They will be mainly working-class youngsters, that's all."

"Will it be good for the village though? I mean, they're not likely to spend much money, are they?"

"It will be excellent for the village in many ways. It will be good for our children to mix with them, at the pool for instance, and get another perspective of life. It will be good for tourism, because if there is an Albergue Juvenil in the village, it will show that we are a bona fide tourist destination. Besides, it won't just be for organised groups. Anyone will be able to stay, if there is room."

"Like hostels in Britain, I guess," said Nigel, remembering his youth hostelling holiday in the Lake District after he had finished his A Levels. That was a far cry from London, but he hadn't got round to venturing further north than Leicestershire since then. "Yes, I'd like to be involved. I think it's the sort of thing I'd enjoy, but I wouldn't expect to be paid much."

"We will set your salary. If you live modestly here, I'm sure you will earn enough not to have to eat into your savings."

"You've given it a lot of thought, haven't you, Enrique?"

"I've thought of nothing else all week. I'm very excited about it, though I may not show it."

"Yes, you have a stiff upper lip, like us British are supposed to have."

"What on earth does that mean?" he asked, feeling his upper lip through his moustache.

Nigel explained.

"Yes, I suppose I have, in some ways. There are aspects of the Spanish character which I don't like. I think we can all learn from each other."

"Without doubt."

"Building work will begin after the summer."

"Who will supervise that?"

"Me, and you, if you like. I will gain permission from the village council to supervise the works."

"And get paid?"

"Yes, though I'll sound out the villagers first. One can't be too careful about these things, but it will be nice to spend less time driving my digger for a few months, unless, that is, you wish to take charge."

"No, no, I know as much about building as I do about filmmaking. In winter I'll spend some time with my mother and sister, and maybe take a trip to North Africa."

At this point Eduardo brought their main dishes, so they chewed in silence for a while.

"Oughtn't I to have an interview for the job I'll be doing?"

"What for?"

"Oh, I don't know, back home that's the way they do things."

"What? Invite people for interview, knowing full well that they aren't going to get the job?"

"That's what they do. It's considered fairer that way."

"It sounds most deceitful to me. The interviewer will need a very... stiff upper lip. No, the village council will vote, and the job will be yours."

"I suppose there'll be a contract to sign."

"Yes, but this is the real contract," Enrique said, stretching his hand over the table.

Nigel shook it, and the tingle he felt reminded him, ever so slightly, of his date with Ana the next day. Things seemed to be falling into place at a vertiginous rate.

The following morning Ana arrived right on time and a few minutes later they were on the open road.

"This car is all right," she said, seeming more relaxed than he had expected.

"Yes, it was a bargain, I hope. I think we'll go to Torrejón El Rubio, if that's all right with you."

"I've heard of it. Where is it?"

"Less than an hour south of here. It's a small village, but has a lot of places for people to stay. I thought it would be interesting to see it, and maybe ask someone how it developed."

"You're very interested in tourism, aren't you?"

"Well, I wasn't, but I guess when I start doing something I tend to take it seriously," he said, glancing at her. She was dressed in jeans, despite the heat, and a plain blue t-shirt which, though not exactly figure-hugging, showed off her assets to good effect. As the old car had no air conditioning, Nigel had decided on shorts, as he would rather look like a tourist than spend the day sweating, and he was rather proud of his legs, which were browner than ever before.

"Did you have a nice lunch with Enrique yesterday?"

"Yes, we had a good chat. A very interesting chat, in fact, but I can't tell you about it just yet," he said, as Enrique had suggested keeping a lid on it until the paperwork had been signed.

"How mysterious! Something good, I hope."

"Yes, I think so."

After hurtling across the plain for twenty minutes the road began to climb into a sparsely wooded sierra, whose higher reaches proved to be more densely forested and stretched away to the east and west. They reached a hamlet called Villareal de San Carlos, so Nigel left the main road to take a look. The place was tiny, but as they strolled around he saw that half of the mainly stone houses had some sort of touristic use. There was a bar, a restaurant, two rural houses to rent, many picnic tables, some under cover of a brand new rustic shelter, and, right in the middle of the only street, the Centro de Interpretación de la Naturaleza del Parque Nacional De Monfragüe.

They walked into the heavily restored stone building and found that it was basically a tourist information centre for the national park.

"Damn it, we should have put this in our leaflet about places to visit," Nigel said.

"Is it too late?"

"Yes, it's at the printers."

"I'll have word with that man over there."

While Ana chatted quietly to the young employee, Nigel marvelled at how they appeared to have made so much of such an unspectacular mountain area. True, there were all kinds of wildlife, such as deer, eagles and vultures, but of the human species there was only him, Ana and the young chap. He had seen a handful of cars in the car park, but he supposed it was the wrong time of year to go tramping in the hills. When Ana approached him with a small cardboard box, they said goodbye to the man and walked out into the sun.

"What's that?"

"Leaflets. We'll just have to put them next to ours."

"Good thinking. Do you fancy a walk?"

"It's far too hot."

"Yes, let's drive on to where we're going."

Soon the road began to descend and after driving over and alongside the River Tagus and negotiating a series of hairpin bends, they found themselves heading out of the forest and back onto the plain.

"It's a nice area, isn't it?" Nigel said, surprised that Ana had never visited it.

"Yes, if I'd known it was there I'd have come before," she replied, which didn't say much for her spirit of adventure, he thought, as they were less than forty kilometres from the village.

"It's pretty, but nothing special really. They've made the most of it though; a good road, that tourist centre, plenty of places to stop to admire the view or have a picnic. That's what rural tourism is all about, showing people what's there right under their noses."

"Yes, I expect for older generations it was of little interest. I mean, if you spend every day outside you don't want more fresh air on Sundays, which was the only day they didn't work. Is this where we're having lunch?" she asked, pointing to the village which had suddenly come into view after a few kilometres of flat, straight road.

"Yes, this is it." He pulled off the road and parked on a wide street, facing numerous small chalets. "It's less than half the size of your village, and not much to look at, but it's teeming with places to stay, or so I read."

"It looks as big as our village."

"Yes, the population used to be over two thousand, until the 1960s, then it gradually dwindled to about six hundred. I think it's starting to grow again now."

"How do you find out all these things, Nigel?" she asked with an especially naïve smile.

"Well, online, on Wikipedia, and other websites."

"Ah, I see."

Dear me, Nigel thought, how little curiosity this girl has. "Let's have a walk around to work up an appetite, shall we?"

"Yes, if you like."

"Look, Apartamentos Rurales Monfragüe. That's four I've seen now, but only one hotel. Apartments seem to be the way forward."

"Yes, I suppose people who come to the mountains and countryside don't mind self-catering."

"I guess that's it, plus they don't have to look at a Eusebio every time they enter or leave," he said, before remembering the principal purpose of the outing. "Of course, if there's someone like *you* in reception, that's a different matter," he added with a smile, edging closer until the sleeves of their t-shirts brushed.

"I'll just be polite in reception. If they wish to chat, I'll chat, but I won't bother them every time they come in," she said, which he thought was missing the point somewhat.

"Shall we find somewhere to eat now?" he asked, hoping that a glass or two of wine might help them to reproduce that heady moment in his house.

They returned to the main road and entered the first restaurant they saw, which was also a casa rural. It was too hot to eat on the terrace, so they went inside to be met by a rather brusque woman who hurried them to a table of her choice and produced the menus.

"She seems to be in a hurry," Ana murmured.

"Or just in a bad mood."

"There is no menú del día today as it is Sunday," she said when she came back two minutes later with a pen and pad.

"I know what day it is," said Nigel, having already dismissed the idea of asking her how the nondescript village had become a tourist destination. Only three other tables were occupied, and he guessed that they were also passing through, and equally ignorant of her charms.

They ordered quickly and were served even more quickly, as the main courses came hot on the heels of the starters, though Nigel's fish was rather cold. Not wanting the dreadful woman to spoil this important lunch, he kept their wine glasses topped up and resolved to ignore her. He tried several topics of conversation, including books, music, travel and pets, in that order, but while

Ana always replied with interest, she never had much to say. Searching desperately for common ground, and after swearing her to secrecy, he told her about the proposed hostel.

"Well, that *is* a good thing, isn't it?" she said with a charming smile.

"Yes, it'll be good for the village, and it'll give me just enough to do, I think. You could work there too, you know."

"Yes, it might be a change from Eusebio's."

"What kind of thing would you like to do?"

"Oh, I don't mind."

"I mean, would you prefer administrative work like you used to do, or reception work, or... something else?"

"I don't mind. Whichever you and Enrique think best."

Nigel topped up her glass, which had yet to become less than two-thirds full, and poured the rest of the white wine into his own.

"You don't seem very ambitious, Ana," he said, patting her hand, just the once.

"No, I'm not really. What I'd really like is to have a family, I suppose."

Having been considering a second pat, he left his hand where it was. Before his half-eaten cold fish could get even colder, the woman came back with the dessert menu.

"Are you expecting a nuclear attack this afternoon?" he asked her with a grave look.

"Qué?"

"You seem to be in a hurry, señora."

"No, no," she replied, looking flustered for an instant, before poising her pen.

"Just a cortado with a drop of brandy for me," said Nigel.

"A café solo for me," said Ana, and the woman was off.

"She's an example of what can go wrong with rural tourism," Nigel said.

"How do you mean?"

"What do you think?"

"Well, I suppose she's just grumpy, that's all."

"Hmm, I think she's followed the lead of other people in the hope of making money, but it's not really for her. She should stay away and let other people run the place," he said, tempering his vehemence with a smile.

"Yes, we don't want that to happen in our village. Although our bar owners have their peculiarities, they all know how to run a bar," she said, lifting Nigel's spirits, not only because she had said 'our village', but because she had actually voiced an opinion.

"Yes, yes, we'll have to be careful about who comes along when things take off."

"Hmm, but you can't stop someone buying a place can you?"

"No, but if anyone like that miserable sow tries to set something up, I might have to use my acting skills and become eccentric again, in order to dissuade them."

"Ha, that would be funny! How would you do it?"

"Oh, let me think... I might warn them about Victor's homicidal tendencies, or tell them what happened to the last outsider who tried to set up a business."

"What would you tell them?" she asked with a delighted and delightful giggle.

"Oh, maybe that they..." He searched for the words. "That they covered him with tar, before sticking feathers all over him. People used to do that in England, you see."

"Really? Have you seen it done?"

Nigel narrowly avoided spitting out his mouthful of coffee. "No, that happened centuries ago, but it sounds pretty gruesome."

"Oh, Nigel, you are funny."

Having got her into a good, slightly dizzy, mood, he decided to get her out of the depressing restaurant as quickly as possible. As soon as she had finished her coffee, he jumped up and called, "Señora, señora!" at the top of his voice.

She hurried in. "Qué pasa?" she asked, looking around her in panic.

"Quick, the bill, we must leave right away!" he cried, tearing at his hair, before winking at the French-speaking people at the only remaining table.

Ironically, it took the woman longer to make up the bill than it had to perform all of her previous tasks, while Nigel paced about, begging her to hurry. When she finally handed it over with outstretched hand and a look of blank astonishment on her face, he slapped two twenties into her palm, took Ana by the hand, and rushed out.

"Oh, she won't forget you!" said Ana, weak with laughter. "And listen to those foreigners laughing."

Without surrendering her hand, he led her away from La Posada el Arriero (take note) and along the deserted road back to the car. The wine, the brandy and, most of all, the rush produced by his theatricals, convinced him that now was the time to get up close and personal. After opening the doors to allow the car to cool down, they got in and he immediately took her hand again. As he thought words – either his or hers – might spoil it, he simple leaned over and kissed her lightly on the lips. Her response surprised him greatly, as she enveloped him in her arms and gave him a proper, prolonged kiss.

When their clinch finally ended and they drew apart, Nigel was tingling from head to foot, but especially in the middle, so what she then said came as a surprise.

"That was nice."

"Yes, it was."

"But it's the last time I'll kiss you."

"Oh."

"We're not compatible, are we, Nigel?" she said, patting his arm.

"Oh, I don't know."

"You know we're not. I'm a simple, home-loving girl and you're, well, you're a bit more complicated. You'd soon get bored of me, and you're not right for me anyway. I hope to meet a nice chap one day soon and if more people come to the village it might happen, but I can't waste my time with you."

"It wouldn't be a complete waste, would it?"

"Of course not, but what if the man for me comes along and I'm still with you? I believe in love, you see, only it's taking a bit longer than I expected."

As the tingling had lessened, Nigel was able to compose his thoughts. "I suppose you're right, Ana. I hate being tied down anyway, so... yes, it's probably best not to... get together."

"Yes, it's best."

"It's a shame though."

"Well, look, if in five years' time neither of us is attached, we could reconsider, couldn't we?" she said with a giggle.

"Hmm, isn't there an expression... amigos con derecho a roce?" he asked, meaning 'friends with a right to brush against each other'.

"There is, but I've never had one and I don't want one now."

"Right, it was just a thought."

"Ha, imagine where I'd be now if I'd taken just a few of those opportunities. I'd be the village harlot."

"Hmm, I suppose it's like that when everyone knows each other. How about a couple of weeks in Morocco this winter?" he asked with a chuckle.

"Not for me, thanks. Come on, let's get back. I told Eusebio I'd pop round to check the bookings."

Their chemical attraction lingered on the drive back, but by the time Nigel pulled up outside the hotel he was resigned to the fact that he and Ana would just be friends, though her five-year plan didn't sound a bad one.

"I'd give you one more final kiss, but I can see Eusebio peering out of the window," she said as she opened the door.

"Better not then. See you later this week, and remember, not a word about the hostel."

"Bye, Nigel, and thanks."

12

That evening Nigel's feelings were of frustration mingled with resignation, but by the following morning only the resignation remained, together with a sense of relief. Ana had been right, of course, and a relationship between them couldn't possibly have prospered, but where did that leave him now? Well, he'd had prolonged celibate periods before, so another one wouldn't hurt him, and there was still Carla, with whom he felt he had much more in common. She would probably ask him about his outing with Ana, as a few people had seen them in the car, but Ana was bound to be discrete, so no-one would know about their single embrace and subsequent decision, or Ana's decision, to avoid further intimacy.

As he was getting ready to go to the pool a little boy called to tell him that the boxes of leaflets had arrived at the village hall, so he picked up his knapsack and walked round there.

"Enrique said to tell you as soon as they arrived," said Marta, the rather taciturn custodian of the village archives, before pointing to two cardboard boxes which were smaller than he had expected. Nigel ripped the tape off the box containing the village leaflets and pulled one out. He saw with relief that the colours and print quality were good, before handing it to Marta. He didn't need to read it, as that very morning he had perused it on his laptop.

"What do you think, Marta?"

"Very nice. Good photos, and easy to read. Yes, they're all right," she said, a great compliment from her, as she was famously unforthcoming, though an efficient administrator.

"Carla's ex-husband took the photos, I think."

"Ah, Mateo, a lovely man."

"Was he?" I mean, is he?"

"Yes, but she drove him away, the silly girl."

Nigel had never thought of Carla as a silly girl – Ana perhaps, but not Carla – though he doubted that Marta would elaborate unless he gave her some encouragement.

"Why silly?" was all he could think of to ask.

"Oh, I don't know. They seemed to be getting on well, then one day it appeared that they weren't, and before we knew it he had gone off to Seville. It was quite sudden, you see, though neither of them had been unfaithful, as far as we knew, and someone would have known, I'm sure. Such a shame, but life's like that," she said with a shrug, before turning back to the computer screen.

Nigel opened the other box and handed her the 'Places to Visit' leaflet, hoping that she hadn't quite exhausted her daily quota of words.

"Hmm, yes, very nice, and useful too. It's surprising how many places there are to visit. I haven't been to Trujillo for years."

"I forgot to put in the Monfragüe National Park, unfortunately."

"Where's that?"

"South of here, about forty kilometres by car."

"What's there?"

"Well, mountains, not very high ones, and… wildlife."

"Hmm, where's the nearest town?"

"Plasencia's the nearest big town. There's just one tiny village in the actual park."

"That's probably why I haven't heard of it." She unfolded the three-page leaflet. "I wouldn't worry about it. There are plenty of places for people to visit in here. Ha, you should send one to every house. Some of the villagers are so uncultured that they probably don't even know Cáceres properly. If they go, they go to the shopping centres." She sniffed and shook her head with disdain.

"I'll go into the council room and have a think about what to do with them all."

"Very well."

After making little piles of leaflets on the table, there seemed to be rather a lot of them after all. He decided to put the 'Places to Visit' leaflets inside the village leaflets, and after doing about three hundred and putting them in his bag, he took his leave of Marta and headed towards Fernando's, before remembering the box of Monfragüe leaflets that he had left at home. Keen to do things right, he went home and spent half an hour slipping those leaflets inside the 'Places to Visit' leaflets, before finally beginning his promotional tour.

"Fernando, I'm going to leave you fifty of these for now," he said upon receiving his café con leche.

"Just pop them near the newspapers."

"I'll leave a few on the bar, but I want you and Eduardo to give them out to the right people."

"Eh?"

"I don't want them to end up in Juan's litter cart, Fernando. I want you to give them to everyone who looks like a tourist."

"Tell Eduardo, I'm not a tourist guide," he said, being in one of his bad moods, which occurred roughly every three days, but always on Mondays, after his day off. This fact struck Nigel, and he decided to include it in his subsequent lecture.

"Fernando, this tourism business is going to be a team effort," he said, cringing inwardly at the words that he had heard so often at work in London, especially when things were going badly. "We all have to do our best to promote it, and I'm not asking much, just to keep your eyes open for people who look like they might come back or tell other people about the village."

"And how am I supposed to know who they are?"

"Look, if a guy comes in dressed in overalls or other work gear, orders a beer, and then goes to play the slot machine, he's probably not interested. If, on the other hand, you see a couple who you don't know and who look sort of interested in the place, give them the leaflets with the bill. Is that too much to ask?"

"All right, but you'd better explain it to Eduardo too, slowly."

"I will. I think you ought to think about opening on Sundays, you know, especially in summer."

"What? Do you want to kill me?"

"No, you could take another day off," he said, before pointing out, as he had to Esteban, that there were students on holiday who would be glad to work behind his bar until September. "Sunday, is *the* day for people to drive out to lunch, Fernando. The other bars open, but they're not proper restaurants. I bet lots of people have stopped here, looked around, and then driven on to have lunch somewhere else." Fernando looked unimpressed, so he changed tack. "I mean, a lot of them will have eaten at Sara's, I'm sure, and they might try Esteban's when he reopens, because he's going to take on more staff for the summer, so I suppose it doesn't matter whether you open or not." He proffered a coin and gazed into Fernando's eyes, which were beginning to look especially hawkish.

He waved the coin away. "I'll think about it," he said, before withdrawing into the kitchen to berate the cook.

After giving Eduardo a succinct leaflet tutorial, Nigel moved on to Esteban's bar. The big man wasn't there, but his father was in his usual place, now seated on one of the old metal chairs.

"Ah, young man, as you can see, we may reopen before I die, after all."

"I'm sure, Sr. Almaraz. I've brought some of the new leaflets."

Unlike Fernando, the old man was intensely interested in their content and began to read them from cover to cover through his thick glasses.

"Very good, Nigel, and very fine photographs," he said about five minutes later.

"I'd like them to be given to the right people. You know, people from elsewhere who might come back, or tell other people about the village."

"Leave them with me. I will take charge of this operation, as my son is too stupid to distinguish between his next-door neighbour and a Japanese tourist."

"Thanks. Oh, do you know the Monfragüe Sierra?"

"Of course, I used to hunt there, but now, alas, it isn't allowed, so they hunt with their cameras instead."

Nigel moved on to Sara's bar, and she said that fifty leaflets wouldn't last long. "I get many people who are passing through, you see, but I won't waste them."

"Gracias, Sara."

"Do you like my new sign?"

"Oh, yes."

"María Dolores, who has the bakery near the library, now wants to get one. She is such a copycat."

"Ha, the more the better."

"I have ordered a new sign," were the first words that Victor uttered when Nigel walked into his den of iniquity, or potential iniquity, as it was almost empty.

"That's great. It'll make a big difference." He looked at the tapas cabinet and spotted a brand new potato omelette. "Can I have some of that and a beer, please?"

As he munched and sipped, Victor read the leaflets.

"Very good, though most of the degenerates who come in here won't be interested."

"Ha, but you get your football crowd in the evenings. During the day you must be ready for passing tourists." He noticed that not only were the tapas very fresh, but that Victor's white shirt was clean, so he decided to say no more. He hadn't eaten a thing there since the night he had impersonated his own twin brother, and Victor watched him devour the omelette with satisfaction. Nigel also noticed that the three-year-old calendar had been replaced by a new one, and that the whole place was considerably cleaner.

"This winter I may close for a few weeks to refurbish the bar."

"Really? That's a good idea."

"Yes, we must look to the future. My son, who studied *engineering*, is now working at a café in Geneva. 'Son,' I said. 'If you have to work in a bar, you might as well come home and work in this one.'"

"And what did he say to that?"

"At first, he laughed, but when I pointed out that I would like to retire five or ten years from now he fell silent, before saying that he would think about it. I also told him that we were soon to become a tourist destination."

"Did he laugh at that too?"

"Not at all. 'About time,' he said. He also said that my bar was a disgrace. Imagine, my own son speaking that way! But, as you can see, things are improving."

"Yes, I can see that."

"Ah, my son had such high hopes, but now he's just like the Spaniards who emigrated in the 50s and 60s, always doing the worst jobs. 'Come home and make something of this,' I said, and I think he will, maybe next year."

"I'm glad. Here are some leaflets. Give them to outsiders who you think might come back."

"I will." He took the small pile. "How many are there?"

"About forty, I think."

"They will last me a while, but a couple from the hotel came for a drink last night. It's fortunate that there is no football in summer."

"They'll get a leaflet at the hotel," Nigel said, before trying and failing to pay, and heading that way.

"I will need a *lot* of leaflets," said Eusebio, who had shot out of reception like a scalded cat when he saw Nigel approaching.

"You can have all these, and I'll bring you some more soon."

"*And* I would like you to design one for the hotel," he said, seeming very chirpy indeed, probably due to the fact that nine rooms were occupied.

"No problem. I'll need some good photos and some ideas for the text."

"Ana and I will sit down to discuss it later. My new chambermaid begins tomorrow. Ana will show her what to do."

"Good."

"Though she seems subdued today."

"Oh."

"After going out with you too. I thought she would be happier."

"Well, it is Monday, after all," Nigel said, looking calmly into his beady eyes.

"She is on the second floor, if you wish to see her."

"Not just now. Please show her the leaflets though. We were talking about them yesterday. Email me the photos and text for your leaflet as soon as you have them," he said in a matter-of-fact way.

"I'll pay you, of course."

"There's no need."

"Ana and I have also been looking at wicker furniture for over there, on the computer."

"Oh, good."

"Ana has very good taste for that sort of thing."

"Yes."

"Much better than me."

"Right."

"You aren't going to tell me anything about your day out, are you?"

"No, Eusebio, I'm not. See you later."

"Adiós, Nigel."

That afternoon Nigel left a few leaflets in all of the shops, giving instructions for their use, but he left the most important shop until last, arriving just before she closed for the day.

"I think they're excellent, and it's a good idea to fold them together like that. I'll leave a few on the counter and keep some more in the drawer."

"Great, do you fancy a quick beer when you close?"

"Well, I really wanted to get home," she said with an apologetic smile.

"That's OK. Listen, are you free next Sunday? You still haven't been for a drive in my new old car yet."

Carla's brow ruffled briefly, before she smiled. "I know, let's go for a quick drive now before dinner. We could stop for a drink at a bar I know in Santibáñez el Bajo."

Although Nigel thought this a strange proposal, as he knew that the village was at least half an hour away, he agreed. When she closed the shop at half past seven, he was waiting in his dusty car and they were soon out in the country, bowling along with the windows down.

"It's getting really hot now," he said.

"Yes, there'll be no respite until September, then a month later the nights will start getting cold again. I'm not surprised that Extremadura is one of the last places in Spain to become a tourist destination. We have very short springs and autumns here."

They spoke little more on the drive to the village, but when they had taken their seats at a table on the terrace of a bar in the quaint little square, Nigel decided to make the most of their time together.

"Ana and I went out for lunch yesterday. We went to Torrejón El Rubio."

"I know. I mean, I know you went out. You can imagine that during a whole day in the shop someone was bound to tell me," she said with a laugh.

"What time did someone tell you?"

"Oh, as I was unwrapping the newspapers. News travels fast there."

"Yes, I know." He sipped his beer and waited for her to speak.

"Did you have a good day?"

"Yes, it was all right. We… we didn't seem to have as much to talk about as me and you though. Do you know the Monfragüe Sierra?"

"Of course. Oh yes, you must have driven over there, thus the leaflet. We missed it out, didn't we?"

"Yes, but not to worry."

"So I take it the outing wasn't a success, Nigel?"

"Well, I wouldn't say that. Like you said, there's no harm in going out, and she's a lovely girl, but... well, like I said, I don't think we have very much in common." He shrugged, sipped and smiled.

"And you think we do, is that it?"

Taken aback but not dismayed by her directness, he drained his glass. "Well, yes, I do. A lot more, in fact," he said, gazing into her sunglasses, which she then took off and slid over her hair.

"I'm afraid there's one thing that we don't have in common. No, hang on, it's something that we *do* have in common, but which presents rather an obstacle." She bit her bottom lip and raised her eyebrows.

"What's that?"

"We both like women."

"Oh." He scratched his chin and looked at the drinking fountain in the middle of the square. "You mean you like women in... that way?"

"Yes, I'm afraid I do."

"But you were married."

"Yes, and I don't dislike men. In fact it was only when I met my friend from Talavera de la Reina that I realised."

"When was that?"

"About two years ago, after Mateo and I had split up, fortunately."

"Yes, I suppose it was, but what would have happened if you'd met her earlier?"

"Who knows? I really don't know. I mean, the little passion that I had for Mateo soon ended, but I'd never thought about women in that way until I met her, though I'd always had a feeling that... well, just a feeling sometime about certain women, but I just reasoned that none of us are entirely heterosexual, deep down."

"I am," he said, managing a grin.

"Ha, I expect you are, but it's not so clear cut for all of us. Marisa and I hit it off right away. We're perfect for each other."

"Was she... is she...?"

"A lesbian? Yes, always, but she's quite pretty, you know."

"I didn't suggest she wasn't," he said with mock umbrage. Though her news had been a shock, he didn't feel at all despondent. It certainly explained a lot, and it dawned on him that he might be about to have what he had never had before; a true, platonic, female friend.

"Anyway, we met in her town when I went to visit my aunt, and one thing sort of led to another."

"Did it take long for you to realise that you were attracted to her?"

"Yes and no. I felt something strange, but she knew, and she just waited till I realised."

"How long did that take?"

"Goodness me, Nigel! This is like the inquisition."

"Sorry, I'm just interested, that's all."

"Well, nothing happened that first time, but the next time I went to visit her – just her, not my aunt – well, we'd had a few drinks and I kissed her, and then it all became clear."

"I see."

"Do you want any more details?" she asked, beaming at him.

"No, no, of course not. What do your family think?"

"Well, that's another matter, and I should have sworn you to secrecy before telling you this."

"I'm a tomb, really I am."

"I hope so. My mother and father know, and a few close friends."

"And Enrique?"

"Yes, and he was very understanding. My uncle is the sort of person who believes that people should follow their instincts."

"I know."

"But it is *not* something I want the people in the village to know about."

"Don't worry." Spotting the waiter, he asked him to refill their glasses.

"And now you want to ask me what my parents thought of it all, don't you?"

"Well, yes."

"Shocked at first, but my mother soon came round; my father too, but more slowly, but he'd hate it if it became common knowledge."

"What will you do then? Just visit each other?"

"No, we have plans. I shall probably go to live with her in Talavera, when I can find someone to manage the shop."

"Don't look at me."

"I wasn't, but there is someone I've thought of."

"Ana?"

"Yes, what do you think?"

"I think she'd be perfect, and it would be perfect for her, though Eusebio would have a fit."

"Oh, it won't be for a while yet. Maybe next winter."

Then something dawned on him. "Does Ana know about your... partner?"

"Oh yes, she's one of the first people I told."

"Ha, you fibber!"

"I thought it best to say we weren't close, at that time."

"So I guess you'll know all about our trip yesterday?"

"Your first and last kiss? Yes, she told me last night. She was quite sad about it, you know."

"Me too, but it's for the best, I think."

"Yes, I expect so, but you never know. I suppose it depends on what kind of wife you want; whether you want a soulmate or a… faithful companion."

"Ana says she believes in love."

"And don't you?"

"I guess so," he said, before deciding to change the subject. "I've got a secret for you to keep too."

"I'm a tomb."

He outlined the plans for the proposed youth hostel.

"That sounds perfect for you, Nigel, I'm so glad," she said, squeezing his hand.

"Perfect for the village too, I hope."

"Yes, that too. Just think about all the people you'll meet, and not just kids from Madrid."

"Yes, a young, rich, intelligent, beautiful woman will walk through the door on our first day, ha ha."

"Ha, maybe, but someone will come along one day. In any case, you and Ana still have your five-year plan."

"Damn it, does she tell you everything?"

"Oh yes. Come on, it's getting dark."

"We must come here again another evening. I've enjoyed out little chat."

"Me too. You know, you *are* nice, Nigel."

"One tries."

Epilogue

One month later Nigel Hamson, doubly spurned lover and soon-to-be manager of the soon-to-be restored youth hostel, was lying on the grass by the local swimming pool. He had just bought his plane ticket to Quebec, where he would spend three weeks with his mother, sister, nephew, niece and brother-in-law, before coming back, after a quick break in Madrid to see Stephen, and getting down to business. In the end Enrique's employer could only spare him one day a week, so Nigel was to help supervise the building work, and liaise with Lourdes regarding the bookings they would take from the following Easter.

Before his trip he still had over a month to kill, and as the hotel and all the bars were running smoothly and benefiting from the small but significant increase in trade – partly thanks to the wooden signs, he always thought – he had begun to read through all the notes he had made in his notebooks. Some things were quite good, he thought, and maybe he'd make the interesting bits into short stories and send them off to a magazine or something. All they could do was reject him, after all, and he was used to that.

As the midday sun was becoming too hot to bear, he pulled on his shorts and t-shirt, rolled up his towel, and made his way to Esteban's bar for a drink before lunch and his now customary siesta. He had spent a lot of time there during the last fortnight, partly in appreciation of Esteban's expensive efforts to improve his bar – which looked very rustic in a new sort of way – but mostly because he had taken to chatting to his father; no longer Sr Almaraz, but Juan Pedro, to him. The old man, whose domino-playing friend was laid low with gout, was a mine of information about how life used to be on the Dehesa Extremeño, or

Extremaduran plains, and Nigel had vague plans to try to write an oral history book based on their conversations.

"Hmm, I see you've brought your little recording device again, young man," he said when Nigel had brought over their glasses of wine.

"Yes, but I won't switch it on if you don't want me to."

"Oh, I have no secrets. Switch the thing on, if it gives you pleasure." The old man smiled on seeing the green light, because he loved to be recorded. "Anyway, what have you been doing with yourself?"

"Oh, lazing about by the pool and thinking about writing something."

"That book about me that you mentioned?"

"No, we need to talk much, much more before I can start that."

"Ha, then I'll be dead before it's finished!" He drank half of his wine.

"Juan Pedro, you're eighty-two and in excellent health. You'll live for years."

"He'll outlive *me*, the old goat," said Esteban from his busy bar. In among his regular patrons there was a young, blond, camera-laden couple with whom he had been ingratiating himself.

"Old Jose Ramón is almost dead," Juan Pedro said to Nigel.

"Jose Ramón has gout. He'll be back here before you know it, and I want to speak to him too. Yesterday you were telling me about the year after you got married."

"What? Oh yes, 1956, the year Real Madrid first won the European Cup." He smiled and adjusted his dentures with his tongue.

"Did you watch it on television?"

"On television? On television, he says! Ha, there were no televisions here then, thank God," he said, scowling at the adverts on the flat screen above the bar.

"Anyway, what was going on around here at that time?"

"Around here? Poverty and hunger. After reading about Madrid's victory I felt like eating the newspaper. Oh, I don't want to talk about that today, Nigel. Talk to me about something else. What are you going to write?"

"I don't know, something about my time here, I guess."

"Yes, write it all down, from your first day until now. That would be very interesting. Yes, you can read it to me."

"I write in English though."

"Then you can translate as you speak. We'll have plenty of time, if I'm still… yes, we'll have plenty of time."

"Hmm, I suppose I could try. Start from the beginning and see how it goes."

"Yes, you do that, then every day you can read me what you've written and I'll tell you if it's any good."

"Thanks, Juan Pedro, that would be most helpful."

Later on, when he had made his post-siesta coffee, he played back the short recording, and though there was no oral history to listen to, it did inspire him to open his notebook at the first page. He then opened a new document on his laptop and wrote the following words:

Even after a week in the village no-one knew exactly where he came from or what he was doing there…

THE END

Printed in Poland
by Amazon Fulfillment
Poland Sp. z o.o., Wrocław